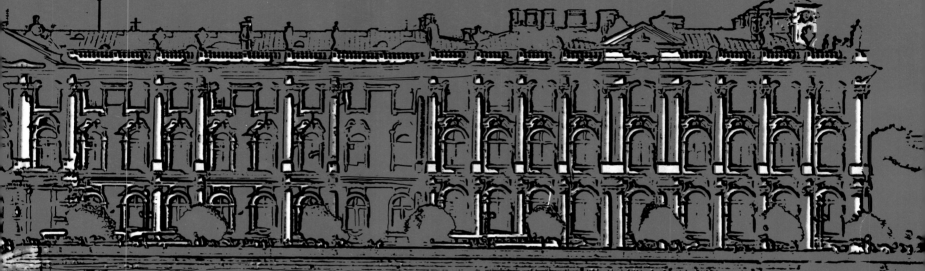

THE HERMITAGE

THE HERMITAGE
Its History and Collections

BORIS PIOTROVSKY

Foreword by Giulio Carlo Argan

Johnson Reprint Corporation
Harcourt Brace Jovanovich, Publishers

Photographs were taken especially for this volume by:

Dmitri Belous: the Hermitage buildings and interiors; nineteenth century watercolors of the Hermitage buildings and the Winter Palace; the Departments of the History of Primitive Culture, Antiquities, and the History of Oriental Culture; drawings, sculpture, applied art, and jewelry of the Department of Western European Art; applied art of the Department of the History of Russian Culture; the Department of Numismatics;

Ivan Pronin and Leonard Heifits: Italian, Spanish, Low Countries, Flemish, Dutch, German, English, and Russian painting;

Leonid Bogdanov: French painting;

Ferdinand Kuzyumov: the Arsenal;

with the participation of Grigori Semenov, a consultant to Academician Boris B. Piotrovsky.

Captions for the illustrations were compiled with the participation of Grigori Semenov and the Museum staff, and are based on the *Catalogue of Western European Painting in the Hermitage,* 2nd ed., Volumes 1 and 2 (Leningrad, 1976 and 1981), and on other publications prepared by Museum staff.

English edition translated from the original Russian
by Ludmila N. Lezhneva and edited by Patrick Creagh.
Designed by Franco Bulletti.
Bibliography prepared by Pietro C. Marani.

Copyright © 1981 by Iskusstvo, Moscow
Giunti Martello Editore, Florence

English translation copyright © 1982
by Johnson Reprint Corporation

Library of Congress Catalog Card Number 82-71739
ISBN 0-384-46420-3

Printed in Italy

First edition

Contents

Bartolomeo Francesco Rastrelli.
Winter Palace entrance
seen from Palace Square.

On the following page:
The Hermitage
from the Palace Embankment.

Foreword

Giulio Carlo Argan

The establishment of a great museum is always a matter of crucial importance, and not only to the cultural world of the country in which it happens to be. The development of the Hermitage has been not so much an effect as a determining cause of the transformation of old holy Russia into an increasingly modern country that is interested in finding and understanding its relations with the West, and that is culturally restless and beset by ever deeper social changes. With the breakup of the traditional theocracy there began a process of secularization and cultural updating that has led the Russian people to an awareness of their own genuine history, far more profound and complex than the version traditionally presented as the ritualistic transmission of political and religious power.

The first phase in the growth of the museum was the original massive assembling of Western works of art ordered by the "enlightened" rulers of the eighteenth century, and particularly Catherine the Great, with a view to Westernizing at least the life of the court. This sudden vertical ascent, so to speak, was followed by a phase in which the museum, though remaining under the control of the czar, was managed by specialists who represented the new middle-class culture: the same sort of people who throughout the enormous territories of Russia undertook systematic archaeological research leading to the discovery of remote and forgotten civilizations. Since the middle of the last century the Hermitage has been the only museum to assemble an organic documentation of the lost civilizations of northern Europe and Asia, making discoveries that, as we are well aware, have changed not only our legacy of information, but also the methods of research employed in archaeology and art history.

The third phase, one that started with the October Revolution, is still in progress. When the museum became the property of the Russian people, it also received the fabulous collections of the aristocratic families. Since then archaeological studies have multiplied, research has evolved, methods of cataloguing have improved, and ways of preserving and protecting this legacy of monuments and art treasures have been modernized and perfected.

The Hermitage is also the only one of the world's great museums to have been established in intimate connection with the founding of a capital city. When Peter the Great founded Petersburg in 1703, with its rational layout and buildings that anticipated the full flood of the Enlightenment, he had a precise aim in mind: to free the government and the state institutions from the intrusive, oppressive, and reactionary influence of the Orthodox clergy, whose center of power was Moscow. To turn Russia into a secular state obviously meant Westernizing it, cutting the dominant caste down to size, opening the country up to the ideas and ideologies of the Enlightenment, transforming the economics of land tenure, and developing craftsmanship according to the new and most advanced techniques, the models for which were to be found in the West. This operation required new structures, and of these the Hermitage was without doubt the most important. Until then the czars had shown no interest in or sensitivity toward art. Their treasure house certainly contained a myriad of fabulous pieces, but it was more like Ali Baba's cave than a royal collection. Only at the time of Catherine the Great was any attempt made to catalogue the material, classify it, put it in order, fill in the gaps, and make any sense of the collection as a whole. By the end of the eighteenth century, the Hermitage had become a true museum of the Enlightenment, in which all schools of art were impartially represented—at the time, a novelty even in Europe, where most museums were based on a nucleus from the collections of kings or noblemen. The Hermitage was, in short, the first museum born of the art market as we know it today, which gave it an air of absolute modernity.

The conspicuous buying campaigns carried on by the czars through their ambassadors and emissaries in Western Europe constitute an interesting phenomenon even in the context of the economic history of the eighteenth century. Behind the façade of cultural liberalism and patronage prevalent at the Russian court lay a play of financial investment aimed ultimately at reforming culture and customs—especially customs. In these same years the czars sent to Italy, France, and Germany for the architects who would give the new capital a look that was less Russian—in fact, as European as possible; of this undertaking, the works of art were the logical complement.

Western Europe was beginning to feel the economic crisis ultimately brought about by the inevitable cost of progress. In Russia, of course, the living conditions of the poorest classes were even more desperate, yet the autocratic regime allowed an exploitation still more pitiless than that in the West. The "enlightened" monarchs—including Catherine the Great, who spent vast sums to acquire art works in the European 9

markets—constantly issued decrees that, to increase the income of the state, worsened the already tragic situation of the peasants and serfs. Catherine could boast of having secured a large batch of pictures that Frederick the Great wanted but could not afford to buy from the German merchant Johann Ernest Gotzkowski, but in fact it was the downtrodden peasantry whose sacrifices paid for the works of art that were to Westernize and secularize Russian culture. Ironically those works—the purchase of which was advised by intellectual giants of the West such as Diderot, who corresponded with the enlightened despots—in the long run nourished in Russian minds a longing for freedom that drove them to get rid of all despots, enlightened or otherwise, forever.

It is common knowledge that the desire to reform the system was overwhelmed by strong reaction: the absolutism of the czars turned inward and became fruitless, the court lapsed in ignorance and bigotry, and the capital was shifted back to Moscow. But the growth of the Hermitage did not stop. Just as a collection destined for Frederick had been snapped up in 1772, so in 1814 the Hermitage acquired 118 paintings that had belonged to Empress Josephine.

In the nineteenth century the management of the imperial collections was transferred from court officials to scholars, and in 1852 Nicholas I, partly to rid himself of the expense of the Hermitage's upkeep, handed it over to the state. A public museum at last, the Hermitage now came within the sphere of

that middle-class culture nourished by the Enlightenment: a culture that on the one hand gave birth to the first courageous freedom movements and later to revolution, and on the other hand—though not without close idealistic links with the former—gave rise in nineteenth-century Russia to an extraordinary pleiad of novelists, philosophers, scientists, and musicians.

The new intelligentsia also attempted to forge links with the West, particularly with Republican France. At the same time, however, it was painfully involved in defining its own historical identity, searching deep into the past in an attempt to understand not only the feelings and natural tendencies but also the genuine history of the Russian people. The result was early studies of the language, folk traditions, and religious beliefs of the various peoples who made up the Russian "nation," the limits of which were certainly not easy to define. It was this need to find out more about the ethnic and historical context that prompted the first expeditions and research north of the Black Sea and in Siberia and Mongolia. These scientific explorations revealed evidence of the art of civilizations that were remote and almost forgotten—or rather, mixed up in a vague concept of the "barbarous," which was then quite arbitrarily set against the ideal of the "classical." From this came the complex but distinct notion of a Nordic art, very different in its structures from the art of the Mediterranean, with which it had had frequent and intense relations. This surprising docu-

mentary material enabled scholars such as Josef Strzygowski and Wilhelm Worringer to cite an anticlassical alternative to what came to be considered a continuous tradition of classicism endowed with eternal values, which coarse intrusions of "barbarism" could only superficially disturb.

In addition, this line of inquiry fit in with Alois Riegl's research into the late Roman *Kunstindustrie* and the ornate art of the late ancient and Byzantine periods—that is, research into the infiltration of "official" classical art by provincial and even downright "barbarous" iconologies and morphologies, and the life these brought to a courtly and oratorical tradition that was becoming increasingly rigid and repetitive. Needless to say, the research begun during the last century under the auspices of the Petersburg Academy of Sciences and the Imperial Archaeological Commission has been continued and intensified since the October Revolution by the Archaeology Institute of the Academy of Sciences of the U.S.S.R.

The time of the great purchases of vast lots of pictures on the Western markets may well seem the golden age of the Hermitage. Purchases such as the collections of Count Brühl, Lord Walpole, and above all Pierre Crozat (with a Raphael and a Giorgione, to cite only two of the masterpieces included) are events that have no parallel in the whole of the eighteenth century. To find any similar cultural transmigration, one must await the establishment of the great American museums in the second half of the nineteenth century and the beginning of the

twentieth—an analogy less superficial than might appear at first sight. No less important was the development of the Hermitage during the second half of the last century, when block purchases gave way to acquisitions only of works carefully chosen and sought out by the directors, who by that time had all the expertise and experience of the connoisseurs of the West. We need only mention two extraordinary masterpieces by Leonardo, the *Madonna Litta* purchased in 1866, and the *Benois Madonna* acquired in 1914. The best proof of the scientific character of the museum's recent management is the acquisition of the splendid collection of drawings, including architectural and scenographic works.

The flowering of archaeology and art history studies in this century and the last has given the Hermitage the air of an encyclopedia of art, even if the stress is still on Western European art and the ancient Scythian, Sarmatian, Siberian, and Mongol civilizations. There are also Egyptian, Coptic, Assyrian, Byzantine, Persian, and Far Eastern sections. The entire artistic culture of the immense continent of Asia is represented as in no other museum in the world. Interesting indeed is the implied comparison with the vast amount of material on the Greco-Roman world: the two famous old collections of Brown and Campana and the huge assembly of painted vases, jewelry, cameos, woven materials, and goldwork.

The October Revolution brought about yet another qualitative leap in the development of Russia's greatest 11 museum. Contributing significantly was the change that had taken place in middle-class culture during the nineteenth century. It was a question of choosing between the backward traditionalism of the court and clergy, which saw the spark of revolution in every cultural novelty, and the industrial progress of Western Europe, which in spite of its inner turmoils necessarily and inevitably implied social progress. The rising middle class saw its future prospects thwarted by a regime hostile to any sort of progress. Partly as a reaction to the obtuse imperialism that had led Russia into the stupid and disastrous war against Japan, this advanced and forward-looking middle class identified more and more with the most highly industrialized Western countries—not so much Germany, which was friendly with the czar, as Republican France. Never had there been such a thrust toward Western culture in its most extreme forms.

Toward the end of the nineteenth century, Russia produced a modernist and symbolist art movement that by the second decade of this century had evolved into a courageous and extremist avant garde: the movement that about 1920, led by Mayakovsky, produced the great art of the Revolution. It is true that a number of Russian artists, to mention only Kandinsky, Malevich, and Chagall, had received their artistic education in the West, particularly in Paris and Munich. But even this must be linked with the development of the Soviet museums, which had acquired great recently formed collections such as those of Kushelev-Bezborodko, Stroganov, and Yusupov. Some of these, such as Shchukin's and Morozov's, were devoted chiefly to the impressionists and to the great French artists of the early twentieth century—Picasso and Matisse, among many others.

The reactionary coalition that tried desperately to smother the revolution and restore the czarist autocracy in Russia imposed tremendous sacrifices on the country, including the sale abroad of a number of works of art, some of them from the Hermitage. In return, however, the private collections passed into the hands of the public, and the Hermitage had to find new space not only for them, but also for the new and often astonishing results of the archaeological expeditions.

The Hermitage today is the great modern museum of a great modern country. Scientifically organized and run, it has an administrative staff far larger than most Western museums. It is equipped with first-class facilities for restoration, cataloguing, photographic records, teaching, and the arrangement and exchange of exhibitions. It is also a center of study—not simply the place where archaeological finds are gathered and displayed, but the organism that promotes the research in the first place. Collaboration and exchange with the great museums of Western Europe, and particularly with Italy, have become increasingly vigorous and productive; in fact, an agreement was recently made to establish "twinship" with the Uffizi in Florence. This is not simply a significant event, but a symbolic bridge between one of the supreme centers of humanistic and classical culture, and a great museum of Eastern European, Asian, and Middle Eastern culture. Moreover, this pact of brotherhood between the two museums is a commitment to cultural collaboration—specifically, collaboration in all sectors of a modern museum's activities and problems, ranging from methods of conservation and cataloguing to the formation of scientific administrative teams; from restoration techniques to teaching, and the organization of a museum's social function; from methods of display to the museum's necessary relations with advanced studies in archaeology and art history.

Pendant
(of the kind known as *kolt*).
Gold and enamel. 5.1 × 5.7 cm.
Eleventh to twelfth centuries.
From a treasure found in Kiev
near St. Sophia Cathedral in 1885.
In the Hermitage since 1888.

Inner court of the Winter Palace.

Carlo Bartolomeo Rastrelli.
Bust of Peter the Great. 1723–30.
Bronze. 102 × 90 × 40 cm.
The sculptor was the father of
the architect Bartolomeo Francesco
Rastrelli. Transferred from the
Petersburg Academy of Fine Arts in 1848.

Introduction

The Hermitage stands in the very center of Leningrad, on the left bank of the Neva River opposite the Fortress of Peter and Paul. The museum is composed of five buildings dating from the eighteenth and nineteenth centuries, all the work of distinguished architects, and in spite of a diversity of styles they form a harmonious architectural whole.

These buildings are the Winter Palace, the work of the Italian architect Rastrelli (1762); the Hermitage proper (or Little Hermitage), which stands beside it, built to the designs of Vallin de la Mothe in 1769; the Old or Great Hermitage, completed in 1787 by Felten for the express purpose of housing the rapidly expanding collection of pictures; the Theater designed (also in 1787) by Quarenghi, erected on the site of Peter the Great's Winter Palace and joined to Felten's building by a gallery running over the Winter Canal; and finally the New Hermitage, built in 1851 to the designs of Leo von Klenze, architect of the Alte Pinakothek in Munich. The New Hermitage faces onto the street running parallel to the Neva Embankment, and its monumental portico is adorned with ten granite statues of Atlas, the work of the sculptor Aleksandr Terebenev. The interiors of the various buildings are also of great historical interest, as they bear eloquent witness to the taste of the times in which they were built.

The Hermitage collections are truly immense: more than 2,700,000 pieces are divided among the six departments, each of which could easily be a separate museum. The 353 display halls open to the public are distributed among all the above buildings with the exception of the Theater, and there are countless storerooms accessible to students and scholars.

The Hermitage, one of the most famous museums in the world, is a "must" for all visitors to Leningrad. Three and a half million people pass through its halls annually. Each year there are 32,000 guided tours, while lectures are given daily in the Theater. Staff members deliver more than a thousand lectures a year in the most remote areas of the country, including the Far East and Central Asia, bringing knowledge of the museum's treasures to people far and wide. Moreover, the Hermitage regularly mounts exhibitions from abroad and, in turn, sends some of its own treasures on tour, thus contributing to international cultural collaboration.

The Hermitage collections are growing constantly, not only because of acquisitions made in the Soviet Union and abroad, but as a result of archaeological studies. The museum staff undertakes archaeological research on its own and also participates in expeditions organized by the Academy of Sciences of the U.S.S.R. and the individual Soviet republics. Particular attention is given to the artistic education of children, which special recreational and study sections promote.

The reader may wonder how the Hermitage came to acquire its name. In the great palaces of eighteenth-century Europe it was the custom to build isolated pavilions that were called "hermitages" because they were places of retreat. Usually they had two floors, the lower one for the servants and cooks and the upper one for the guests, who were generally few in number. No servants waited on the guests, for the tables were laid in advance and the dishes were sent up in dumbwaiters. There is one such hermitage at Peter the Great's residence at Petrodvorets (Peterhof) on the Gulf of Finland, and another in a copse near Catherine the Great's palace at Tsarskoe Selo (called Pushkin today).

Around the Winter Palace in Petersburg there were no gardens, only parade grounds. The gardens in front of the palace and the Admiralty today were not created until the nineteenth century. Catherine the Great commissioned Vallin de la Mothe to plan a garden and a hermitage at the second-floor level, similar to the one at Tsarskoe Selo and another then to be found at Czarina Elizabeth's old Winter Palace. The garden ran from the empress's private apartments down to the road along the Neva, and at the far end there was a small building, the hermitage, which contained two dining tables, each accommodating six people. The walls were hung with ninety-two paintings from the Winter Palace gallery, which had been founded in 1769 upon the arrival of an art collection from Germany. When this structure was enlarged by Felten's wing and joined to the Theater, the name Hermitage came to be applied to all the buildings in which pictures were hung. Catherine the Great used the word "hermitages"—naturally with the French pronunciation—for the parties she gave for a select circle at court. These took place either in the pavilion or in the apartment in the bridge over the Winter Canal, which joined the picture gallery to the Theater.

It has been a long, hard road from a small royal picture gallery, available to a select few, to a museum that conserves, studies, and displays the treasures of world culture for all who care to see them. Only at the beginning of the nineteenth century did the Hermitage acquire a permanent staff, and permission to visit it could still be obtained only from the palace.

In spite of this, the museum even then began to assume an increasingly important role in the history of Russian culture. A great number of painters and sculptors were able to admire, study, and copy the works of the great masters. The Russian painter Pavel Fedotov recalled that on the emperor's orders one had to wear full-dress uniform to visit the Hermitage. Even as late as 1852, when the New Hermitage was opened as a "public museum," the palace administration remained in charge of the sale of tickets. The main entrance, though awesome with its granite caryatids, had not been designed to accommodate a vast influx of people. By the entrance to the lobby there was a primitive kind of abacus; the doorkeeper used to count people as they arrived and admit them in groups of ten.

In 1914, the year when the First World War broke out, the Hermitage was visited by about 180,000 people. Guided tours had been proposed, but the director refused on the grounds that the museum should be open only to those with sufficient knowledge of the arts. In spite of this, the trade unions had organized visits; in 1913, *Pravda* (founded two years earlier) advised the metal workers on how best to visit the museums of Petersburg, the Hermitage in particular.

The October Revolution brought a radical change. Only a few days after the revolution itself a series of decrees was issued on the preservation of historic monuments. The Winter Palace, until then residence of the czars, was declared a museum like the Hermitage, and in time was completely absorbed by the latter, which in the meantime had been considerably enlarged. Many leading scholars lent their services to the museum, and the Hermitage soon became a very important center of research.

During the First World War the most priceless works were evacuated to Moscow, returning only in 1920. In 1922 all the old exhibition halls were renovated, and large-scale works began to enlarge the museum. New sections were added as a result of the absorption of the Winter Palace, which required overall renovation.

16   In 1914 the museum had sixty-six exhibition halls at its

disposal, chiefly in the Little Hermitage and the New Hermitage, since most of the Felten building had been handed back to the palace administration, and the second floor had been turned into quarters for guests of the imperial court. The works displayed in the New Hermitage were arranged in logical order with the ground floor occupied by works from the ancient world, and the second floor by the picture gallery. The ground floor of the Felten building—vacated by the Council of State, which had been transferred to the Mariinsky Palace opposite the Cathedral of St. Isaac—was crammed with new acquisitions without any semblance of order—Oriental art, antiquities, and arms and armor all jumbled together. When the Winter Palace was annexed to the museum, a far more rational arrangement became possible.

Between 1935 and 1941 the museum was restructured and divided into six great departments: the History of Primitive Culture, Antiquities, the History of Oriental Culture, Western European Art, the History of Russian Culture, and Numismatics. The Arsenal, which houses the collection of arms, formed an independent section of the museum.

Certainly the largest and even today the most famous department is the one devoted to the art of Western Europe. It consists of a wonderful collection of paintings, and also drawings, sculpture, and applied arts. All this was later enlarged and enriched by a great number of French nineteenth- and twentieth-century paintings from the Moscow Museum of Modern Western Art, originally based on the private collections of Morozov and Shchukin. In this way the Hermitage acquired works of the French impressionists and of the schools that followed them.

Next, the restoration staff was considerably enlarged, and new methods were evolved for the care and restoration of pictures, applied art, and antiquities. A large scientific and educational staff was also organized for the benefit of visitors, whose number increased year by year. This staff worked out the best methods of conducting guided tours and art-appreciation classes. All the Hermitage guides were specialists in art history.

In 1941 the activities of the Hermitage were disrupted by the Second World War. In the incredibly short time of one week, about half a million of the most precious items were evacuated once more, this time to Sverdlovsk. But in Leningrad there remained a great deal to do in order to safeguard the buildings and the treasures that had not been removed. Bombproof shelters were constructed in the cellars of the Winter Palace and the New Hermitage to house not only the works of art that remained but also a work force of some two thousand people, including museum employees, painters, and artists. The architect Aleksandr Nikolsky, who during the war lived in the Hermitage, has left us a collection of drawings vividly recording the life and work there of those years.

Even during the siege of Leningrad, however, lectures were given on art and literature, such as the conferences held to mark the eight-hundredth anniversary of the Persian poet

Nizami and the five-hundredth anniversary of the poet Alisher Navoi, the father of Uzbek literature. Then, with the end of the war, came the first steps in a long and difficult restoration both inside and out. All the windows had been broken during the siege, so that snow had severely damaged the mosaic floors and the stuccoes. Work proceeded with speed and efficiency, thanks to the best restorers in the country, who had already worked wonders in rebuilding the ruined palaces on the outskirts of Leningrad, especially at Pavlovsk and Pushkin (Tsarskoe Selo).

By 1950 the Hermitage had been completely restored, and its research and publishing activities began to expand enormously. Numerous scientific works were published on various aspects of world culture, while the Aurora Publishing House and a number of foreign publishers produced lavishly illustrated books on the museum's treasures.

In 1955 1,448,000 people visited the museum; ten years later, 2,385,000. In 1975 the figure reached 3,487,000, a level still maintained in 1980. This growing popularity can be explained not only by a mounting public interest in culture but also by the enormous development of tourism in Russia.

Many priceless treasures, architectural and artistic, perished during the Second World War, but what remains is far more precious still. In 1976 a law was promulgated in the Soviet Union providing for the defense of the country's historic and cultural heritage and the use to which it should be put. Besides this, various public and government organizations are constantly at work to ensure their conservation, in accordance with the UNESCO statute of November 1945 concerning the defense and conservation of the cultural legacy of the human race. The Hermitage has made and is making a vast contribution to this process. The visitor is not always aware of the specialized work involved in the scholarly analysis of the different collections. The museum's experts labor to establish the origin and authorship of each work, to decipher ancient texts, and to compile and edit the museum's scholarly publications.

By conserving and studying the treasures of world culture and making them accessible to all, the Hermitage performs an essential educational role. Its massive entrance doors are open to all who are eager to see its treasures.

St. Theodore Stratilates.
Mosaic icon.
9 × 7.4 cm.
Byzantium, first third
of fourteenth century.
Acquired from the
Bazilevsky collection, 1885.

The Buildings and Exhibition Halls of the Hermitage

In the mid-eighteenth century the site where the five buildings of the Hermitage now stand was occupied by private dwellings. To the east of the Admiralty stood Czarina Elizabeth's Winter Palace; to the west, near the Winter Canal, was the third of Peter the Great's Winter Palaces. Between them were seven private houses belonging to aristocrats, admirals, and generals, as well as the court laundry.

The oldest of the five buildings now occupied by the Hermitage is the Winter Palace, designed by the Italian architect Bartolomeo Francesco Rastrelli. He was originally commissioned, in 1752, to enlarge Elizabeth Petrovna's Winter Palace opposite the Ad-

Bartolomeo Francesco Rastrelli.
Winter Palace. 1754–62.
View from Palace Square.

miralty, but was later authorized to demolish five private houses and design a completely new building. The palace was finished in the spring of 1762, but as Elizabeth had died a few months earlier it passed into the hands of Czar Peter, and almost immediately afterward to Catherine the Great, who ordered the completion of the interiors. Rastrelli left Russia after the palace revolution that brought Catherine into power, but he had time to design the main staircase and the throne room.

Although the empress was already in residence, work continued on the interiors under such leading architects as Jean-Baptiste Vallin de la Mothe, Antonio Rinaldi, and Yuri Felten, joined in 1779 by the Italian architect Giacomo Quarenghi, who did a great deal of imposing work. Among those who worked on the Winter Palace during the first quarter of the nineteenth century were Carlo Rossi, Auguste Montferrand, and Vasili Stasov.

On December 17, 1837, a huge fire destroyed all the interiors of the Winter Palace except the bare walls, but a statute of December 29 ordered the reconstruction of the palace and the renovation of the interiors, a task entrusted to Stasov and Aleksandr Bryulov. By March 1839 the reconstruction of the ceremonial apartments had been completed, and in November of the same year the palace once more became the residence of the Russian emperors. But the restoration of the private rooms, entrusted to the architect Andrei Stakenschneider, took a great many years.

The Revolution of 1917 gave the Winter Palace to the people, and it became a part of the Hermitage. The palace's many reconstructions and renovations had considerably altered its appearance, but in 1925–26 a thorough restoration was carried out. Above all, Rastrelli's splendid gallery, which ran the length of the façade on the first floor, was freed of later additions. Further major restorations, designed to reinstate the work of the great architects of the past, were carried out after the Second World War. These at the same time successfully healed all the building's war wounds, so that the palace emerged in all its former beauty.

Although the southern façade of the Winter Palace, facing the Palace Square, must be considered the principal façade, the main staircase was constructed near the entrance opening onto the Neva Embankment. Designed in the baroque style by Rastrelli himself, it rose the entire height of the building. At first it was made of wood, with walls and columns of fake marble, and was embellished by a host of gilded statues. After the fire of 1837, however, it was rebuilt by Vasili Stasov, who retained its original appearance and scarcely altered the stone portions, but replaced the frail columns of the upper gallery with granite supports. In the eighteenth century the staircase was called the Ambassadors' Staircase, because ambassadors used it to gain access to the ceremonial apartments; later, after the consecration of the Neva River, it was called the Jordan Stair.

A doorway in the upper gallery leads to the ceremonial chambers on the second floor, which run along the side of the palace overlooking the river. These include the Anteroom, designed by Giacomo Quarenghi in 1793 and rebuilt by Stasov after the fire;

Bartolomeo Francesco Rastrelli.
Winter Palace.
View from Palace Square.

Little Hermitage and Winter Palace seen from Khalturin Street.

Bartolomeo Francesco Rastrelli.
Winter Palace entrance
seen from Palace Square.

the Great Room (1,103 square meters, the largest of the ceremonial halls), which Quarenghi created by joining together three smaller chambers (Vasili Stasov renovated it and gave it a more sumptuous appearance); and the Concert Hall, which bears the imprint of both these architects.

The door at the side of the upper gallery of the main staircase leads to the Hall of the Field Marshals (constructed by Auguste Montferrand in 1833–34, once again by uniting three rooms), and through this to Peter's Memorial Hall or the Little Throne Room, dedicated to Peter the Great and designed by Montferrand with a particular wealth of ornament. The walls

of this room are lined with red velvet decorated with two-headed eagles embroidered in silver thread (Lyons work dating from 1857). In a niche above the silver throne, made in London in 1731, is the painting *Minerva and Peter,* the work of Jacopo Amigoni (c. 1730).

A door leads from the Little Throne Room into the Hall of the Coats of Arms, originally designed by Rastrelli as a gallery and later enlarged by Yuri Felten, who added a wing to the courtyard. A balcony supported on double fluted columns with Corinthian capitals runs all the way around this room. At first only the flutings of the columns were gilded, but later this gilding was extended to the whole, giving the

Yuri Felten.
Old or Great Hermitage.
1771–87.

room a particularly solemn appearance. The candelabra and other ornamental features of the room, nearly all of which have now been lost, were decorated with the coats of arms of the Russian governors, whence the room takes its name. From this hall there is a passage to the small Guardroom designed by Stasov in 1839, where the changing of the Imperial Guard took place.

A doorway leads from the Hall of the Coats of Arms into the Gallery of the War of 1812, where there are no fewer than 329 portraits of Russian generals who took part in that war, painted by the English painter George Dawe with the assistance of the Russian painters A. V. Polyakov and V. A.

The Hermitage
from the Palace Embankment.

Jean-Baptiste Vallin de la Mothe.
Little Hermitage:
Northern Pavilion. 1764–75.

Yuri Felten and
Jean-Baptiste Vallin de la Mothe.
Little Hermitage:
Southern Pavilion. 1764–76.
Third floor with attic built by
Vasili Stasov. 1840–41.

Golike. The gallery itself was first designed by Carlo Rossi and rebuilt after the fire by Stasov, who tried to retain its original appearance.

Near the gallery is the Great Throne Room or the Hall of St. George, built in 1795 to a design by Quarenghi. Here the marble columns crowned with Corinthian capitals in gilded bronze, the ceiling with its gilded motifs (their pattern repeated in the mosaic floor), the balcony, the massive chandeliers—all combine to create the utmost solemnity. Above the czar's throne a bas-relief depicts St. George killing the dragon. This room was designed by Stasov after the fire of 1837 in the Russian late neoclassical style.

A small passageway between the Gallery of 1812 and the Guardroom leads to the Great Chapel, de-

signed by Rastrelli when the palace was still under construction, which explains the monograms of Elizabeth Petrovna found on the ornamental gilded scrolls in rococo style. During the restoration Stasov tried to retain everything he could of Rastrelli's original architecture, although the decorations in carved wood had to be replaced with *papier-mâché*.

A corridor leads from the chapel antechamber to the ceremonial rooms that overlook the square, of which three are especially worthy of mention. The first is the Hall of Alexander, built in 1839 by Aleksandr Bryulov with clusters of graceful Gothic columns, their capitals bearing acanthus leaves and

Giacomo Quarenghi.
Hermitage Theater. 1783–87.

Winter Canal with
the Raphael Loggias on the left.

Winter Canal.
View of the Neva.

two-headed eagles. The ceiling and upper parts of the walls are covered with heavy and elaborate plaster-work. The medallions on the walls, depicting allegorical scenes of the War of 1812, are reproductions of the work of Fëdor Tolstoy. Also on the wall, framed in wood, is a bas-relief of Alexander I as a Roman warrior and Rodomysl, the Slavic god of war.

At the end of the apartments along this façade are two exceptional rooms, the White Room and the Gold Room. The former was designed by Bryulov in the classical style in vogue in the 1830s, with a great number of framed plasterwork decorations of children at play and large bas-reliefs depicting the ancient gods. The room is painted entirely in white, without any gilding whatever. As its name implies, the Gold Room (also by Bryulov) is laden with gold, particularly since its renovation by W. A. Schreiber, who gilded the walls completely. Originally only the complex reliefs were gold against a white background,

THE NEW HERMITAGE

Leo von Klenze.
New Hermitage,
built by Vasili Stasov. 1839–52.
Portico sculpture of Serdobolye
granite by Aleksandr Terebenev
after Leo von Klenze's drawings.
1844–49.
View from Khalturin Street.

Leo von Klenze.
Portico seen from Palace Square.

View from the southeast.
Watercolor by Luigi Premazzi.
1861.

giving the room an airy grace that is subsequently lost.

Close to these rooms is the Little Boudoir, designed by Bryulov and completed by G. A. Bosset in the rococo style. The walls are lined with red cloth and enhanced by gilded cornices. The seven wall mirrors create a play of light that gives the room an exceptional luminosity.

The White Room is connected to the great stair-way now known as the October Stair because it witnessed the assault on the Winter Palace in October 1917 (November 1917, according to the new calendar). Designed by Auguste Montferrand and rebuilt by Bryulov, this staircase is very severe in style. It once led, by way of the Dark Passage, to the north-west wing of the Winter Palace, in particular to the Rotunda: an austere circular construction, built by Montferrand in 1830, that connects this wing with the ceremonial chambers mentioned earlier—the Anteroom, the Great Hall, and the Concert Hall. Near the Rotunda is the Moorish Room, used as a dining room by the czar and his family, which in turn leads to the most splendid apartments in the whole palace. Among these is the Malachite Room, the work of Bryulov. The eight columns, eight pilasters, and two fireplaces are faced with fine sheets of malachite by the technique known as Russian mosaic, which brings out all the beauty of this stone that has today become a rarity.

The splendor of this room is accentuated by the completely gilded carved doors, the ceiling, and the

26

bases and capitals of the columns. In October 1917 the Malachite Room and the Little Dining Room adjoining witnessed the last meetings of the Provisional Government. On the mantelpiece of the Little Dining Room is a marble plaque bearing the following inscription: "In this room on the night of October 25–26 (November 7–8) of the year 1917, the Red Guards, soldiers and sailors, having seized the Winter Palace by assault, arrested the members of the bourgeois counterrevolutionary Provisional Government." The clock on the mantelpiece still shows 2:10 a.m., the precise hour of this event.

Exactly how the Winter Palace was decorated

As soon as the Winter Palace was finished, Admiral Cruise's house was chosen as the site of the palace stables. At the same time, in 1763, Vallin de la Mothe was commissioned to lay out the garden and design two pavilions, one on the north and the other on the south side of the garden.

Work on the southern pavilion, destined for Count Grigori Orlov, was completed in 1766, after which the construction of the one at the north end began. This, the Orangery, contained a number of rooms for private retreat, hence its name of the "Hermitage" (since known as the Little Hermitage); it was completed in February 1769. The rooms were used to

Bartolomeo Francesco Rastrelli.
Main Staircase of the Winter Palace
(called the Ambassadors' Staircase
in the eighteenth century,
and later the Jordan Stair).
1756–61.
Restored by Vasili Stasov in 1838.
In the central recess
the statue of *Sovereignty* from
the Tauride Palace in Petersburg.

before the fire in 1837 is known only from the architects' plans and from a few paintings. Prior to the reconstruction, the court administration had commissioned Eduard Gau, Konstantin Ukhtomsky, and Luigi Premazzi to do watercolors of many parts of the palace, and these works are reproduced in this book. Meanwhile, to the east of the palace itself, new buildings were gradually being constructed and connected to form a single architectural whole.

exhibit pictures acquired for the palace gallery. As the number of paintings grew, more space was needed, so two galleries were built along the sides of the Hanging Garden, work being completed in 1775. These too were altered in the course of time, especially the eastern one, at the north end of which Giacomo Quarenghi built a small but ornate study.

Even more altered were the interiors on the second floor of the northern pavilion, the Hermitage proper

(or Little Hermitage). Out of a number of smaller rooms the court architect Andrei Stakenschneider made one large hall, leaving only the outside walls intact. This hall, the Pavilion Hall, is a fine example of mid-eighteenth-century eclecticism. With its white marble and wealth of gilding, the hall—in spite of the mixture of styles—gives an impression of airy lightness. The white stone columns rise from the parquet without bases, as in a stage set. This feeling of light-

Bartolomeo Francesco Rastrelli.
Main Staircase of the Winter Palace.

Aleksandr Terebenev.
Allegorical statue of *Justice*
on a wall bracket of
the Main Staircase
of the Winter Palace.
Alabaster. 1839.

Bartolomeo Francesco Rastrelli.
Main Staircase of the Winter Palace.
Another view.

THE WINTER PALACE

Vasili Stasov.
Anteroom. 1839.
Built in the place of
Giacomo Quarenghi's room of 1793.
Watercolor by
Konstantin Ukhtomsky. 1861.

Giacomo Quarenghi.
Grand Hall or Nicholas Hall.
Rebuilt after the 1837 fire
by Vasili Stasov, who preserved
the hall's proportions and
its Corinthian ornament.
Watercolor by an unknown
nineteenth-century artist.

Hall of the Field Marshals.
Watercolor by Eduard Gau. 1866.

Auguste Montferrand.
Hall of the Field Marshals. 1833–34.
Restored by Vasili Stasov in 1839.

ness and transparency is enhanced by the numerous candelabra imported from France. As a finishing touch the architect set four small fountains in the walls, with conch-shaped bowls and delicate little jets of water resembling the Bakhchisarai fountains in the Crimea celebrated by Alexander Pushkin.

Since the Little Hermitage could not hold the whole collection of the Winter Palace pictures, in 1770 it was decided to build a new construction "in line with the Hermitage," subsequently known as the Old or Great Hermitage. Work went on for seventeen years under the direction of Yuri Felten. Without columns or pilasters, the façade was quite severe,

THE WINTER PALACE

Auguste Montferrand.
Peter's Memorial Hall or
the Little Throne Room. 1833.
Rebuilt after the 1837 fire
by Vasili Stasov.

Vasili Stasov.
Hall of the Coats of Arms. 1839.
Built in the place of
Rastrelli's Gallery of Light,
which Yuri Felten had redesigned
in the eighteenth century.

Hall of the Coats of Arms.
Detail.

Carlo Rossi.
Gallery of the War of 1812. 1826.
Restored by Vasili Stasov in 1839.
Watercolor by Eduard Gau. 1861.

33

Great Throne Room or
the Hall of St. George.
Watercolor by
Konstantin Ukhtomsky. 1862.

Decembrists were brought from the Fortress of Peter and Paul to be interrogated. Stakenschneider added porphyry columns and bronze-faced pilasters, a fireplace in lapis lazuli with jasper columns, and doors with tortoise-shell plaques finely inlaid with metal. Above the doors he inset six bas-relief medallions portraying the Russian military leaders Rumyantsev, Potemkin, Suvorov, Kutuzov, Paskevich, and Dolgorukov. Hanging in this room today are the two Madonnas by Leonardo da Vinci.

Until 1885 the first floor was occupied by the Council of State and Council of Ministers, who adapted all the rooms to their own requirements. The

Great Throne Room or
the Hall of St. George.
Begun by Giacomo Quarenghi,
completed in 1795.
Rebuilt after the fire by
Vasili Stasov and Nikolai Yefimov.
1837–42. Opposite the entrance
is a map of the Soviet Union
made of lapis lazuli, rhodonite,
emeralds, opals, rubies, aquamarine,
and various kinds of jasper.
1937–48.

but in keeping with the Little Hermitage. The interiors resembled those of the palace itself, and Giacomo Quarenghi had a hand in their decoration. As we see them today they have been completely transformed.

The Leonardo Room, the largest of the rooms overlooking the Neva, was originally designed by Quarenghi with classical simplicity, but has since suffered the most from alteration. It was here that the

great staircase in the west wing of the Felten building, linking the first floor with the pavilion and the ceremonial apartments on the second floor, became known as the Council of State Staircase. In 1851–60 Stakenschneider altered both the rooms and the staircase according to his own German neoclassical taste, making them more imposing through elaborate ornamentation.

In 1783 Giacomo Quarenghi was commissioned to

Great Throne Room or
the Hall of St. George.

Great Throne Room or
the Hall of St. George.
Details.

1

3

2

4

36

5

design a building continuing the Felten wing that would be patterned after the Raphael Loggias in the Vatican. This project had already been launched by a group of artists commissioned by Catherine the Great. The plan proved excellent, especially as the first part of the loggias was situated close to the Theater that Quarenghi had also built.

The Theater was erected on the site of Peter the Great's old palaces, of which the architect retained the foundations and walls of the most recent—the one reconstructed by Domenico Trezzini in 1726. Excavations in the cellars of the Theater have brought to light some very fine examples of Dutch tiles in blue

3

6

1

2

1. Andrei Stakenschneider.
Winter Garden.
Watercolor by Eduard Gau. 1865.

2. Yuri Felten and
Jean-Baptiste Vallin de la Mothe.
Hanging Garden.
Rebuilt by Vasili Stasov. 1840–44.

3. Jewelry Gallery in the
northern part of the East Gallery.
Watercolor by Konstantin Ukhtomsky.
1861.

4. South Gallery.
Watercolor by Eduard Gau. 1864.

5. East Gallery.
Watercolor by Eduard Gau. 1861.

6. Andrei Stakenschneider.
Pavilion Hall. 1850–58.
The Little Hermitage's most
important hall, built to replace
several rooms designed by
Yuri Felten in the second half
of the eighteenth century.

7. Pavilion Hall.
Detail.

and some Russian ones, all bearing witness to the wealth of decoration in the original palace.

The Auditorium was designed as an amphitheater. It did not have the usual rows of seats or numbered places, and every person was entitled to sit wherever he pleased; Catherine herself usually sat in the second row near the aisle. Simplicity was the outstanding feature of this remarkable chamber. The walls of imitation marble had ten niches containing statues of Apollo and the nine Muses. Above the niches were medallions of some great men of letters, including Molière, Racine, Voltaire, and Sumarokov. The Theater underwent several restorations that greatly

*THE OLD OR
GREAT HERMITAGE*

1. Andrei Stakenschneider.
Council of State Staircase. 1858.
Built by Yuri Felten in the place
of the Oval Hall in the 1780s.

2. Andrei Stakenschneider.
Early Renaissance Art Room. 1858.
Built in the place of a room built
by Yuri Felten in the second half
of the eighteenth century;
rebuilt by Giacomo Quarenghi
in the early nineteenth century.

3, 4. Andrei Stakenschneider.
Suite of rooms of
Early Renaissance Art. 1858.

5. Andrei Stakenschneider.
Leonardo Room. 1858.
Built in the place of
Giacomo Quarenghi's
nineteenth-century Italian Room.

changed its original appearance.

To join the Theater to the wing designed by him, Felten built an arched passageway over the Winter Canal. This bridge contained the foyer of the Theater. In 1904 this foyer was reconstructed by L. N. Benois in the style of 1760, when rococo was giving way to neoclassicism. Paintings by Luca Giordano adorned the ceiling, while above the door was a painting by the eighteenth-century artist Hubert Robert.

In July 1837 a decree was issued for the construction of a new museum, and this project was put in the hands of Leo von Klenze, well-known for his work on art museums in Munich. The south wing next to

the Felten building had to be knocked down to make room for this. In July 1839 Klenze came to Petersburg for the first time, bringing with him a plan he had already drawn up. He proposed to demolish the Little Hermitage, make an open square between the Winter Palace and the New Hermitage now to be built, and remodel the façade of the Felten building. These changes were not accepted, however, so the architect had to design an entrance portico on the south side of the building, keeping the ceremonial entrance on the west side that today opens onto a narrow courtyard.

The portico facing what is now Khalturin Street is embellished with twelve statues of Atlas five meters

tall, which were designed by Klenze and executed by Russian craftsmen under the direction of Aleksandr Terebenev, who personally helped finish each statue. Klenze himself was struck by the high standard and accuracy of these works, which he compared with those of ancient Egypt.

On both the façades of the main entrance, as on the more decorative façade, the windows of the ground floor were replaced by sixteen niches containing large statues of artists and sculptors of antiquity, as well as famous art historians such as Winckelmann. Smaller statues of celebrated artists were placed on the corbels of the west front and the towers at the corners

3

4

5

THE RAPHAEL LOGGIAS

1. Watercolor by
Konstantin Ukhtomsky. 1860.

2. Giacomo Quarenghi.
1783–92.
The frescoes made by Raphael
and his pupils in the
Vatican loggias were copied
by a group of artists under
Christopher Unterberger in 1780.

THE NEW HERMITAGE

3. Leo von Klenze.
Grand Staircase and Entrance Hall.
Watercolor by Konstantin Ukhtomsky.
1853.

4. Ancient Sculpture Room.
Watercolor by Luigi Premazzi.
1856.

5. Greek Sculpture Room.
Watercolor by Konstantin Ukhtomsky.
1853.

6. Leo von Klenze.
Twenty-Column Hall.
Watercolor by Konstantin Ukhtomsky.
1853.

7. Empress's Study, with
a display of Scythian artifacts.
Watercolor by Eduard Gau. 1856.

6

7

43

THE NEW HERMITAGE

Egyptian Sculpture Room.
Watercolor by Konstantin Ukhtomsky.
1858.

Voltaire's Library.
Watercolor by Konstantin Ukhtomsky.
1859. (Now the Antiquities Room.)

Leo von Klenze.
Tent Room. 1842–52.
Built by Vasili Stasov
and Nikolai Yefimov.

Tent Room.
Watercolor by Luigi Premazzi.
1858.

Italian Painting Room
(the Big Skylight).
Watercolor by Eduard Gau. 1853.

Dutch and Flemish Painting Room.
Watercolor by Luigi Premazzi.
1860.

45

of the palace. The New Hermitage, with its portico adorned with gigantic figures, was therefore well suited to the street it faced, and had an imposing appearance in spite of its eclectic style containing elements from classical, Renaissance, baroque, and German neoclassical architecture.

The Atlas portico gave access to the ceremonial stairway leading to the second floor with its great sky-lighted rooms. The upper walls and ceilings of these were covered with elaborate plasterwork.

The architectural plan for the new building was drawn up by Stasov, who headed the commission responsible for the construction of the New Her-mitage. All the interiors of the museum were executed with the direct collaboration of Stasov and Nikolai Yefimov. After Stasov's death in 1848, Yefimov was left in sole charge, and work continued until 1851.

From 1860 on, Gau, Ukhtomsky, and Premazzi, who painted the restored rooms in the Winter Palace, also made some marvelous drawings of the rooms in the New Hermitage, including detailed reproductions of the exhibits of ancient art on the ground floor and the pictures in the second-floor gallery. As many of these drawings are reproduced here, I will not describe the rooms of the New Hermitage, which still retain their original appearance.

1. New Hermitage: Gallery of the History of Ancient Painting. Watercolor by Eduard Gau. 1859.

2. New Hermitage: Engravings Room. Watercolor by Konstantin Ukhtomsky. 1865. (Now the Room of Attic Vases.)

3. English Art of the Seventeenth Century: room in the western wing of the Winter Palace. Interior decoration by Aleksandr Bryulov. 1839.

4. French Art of the Eighteenth Century: the Greuze Room, in the southern wing of the Winter Palace. Interior decoration by Aleksandr Bryulov. 1839.

On the pages following:
French Art of the Seventeenth Century: the Poussin Room, in the southern wing of the Winter Palace. Interior decoration by Aleksandr Bryulov. 1839.

46

The Department of the
History of Primitive Culture

The Department of the History of Primitive Culture (the archaeology of Eastern Europe and Siberia) was set up in 1931. It houses the results of archaeological excavations throughout the Soviet Union, with the exception of antiquities from the Transcaucasian republics, Central Asia, and the Greco-Roman colonies along the north coast of the Black Sea, which are preserved in the Oriental and Antiquities departments. There are also small collections of archaeological materials from other countries.

Most of the items brought together here belong to epochs predating national states, or to the period when these states were coming into being. Occasion-

Female statuette.
Mammoth ivory. Height 16.6 cm.
Malta culture, 20,000 B.C. Site
of Malta, near Irkutsk, Siberia.
Excavations by M. M. Gerasimov, 1929.

Figurines of birds.
Mammoth ivory.
Malta culture, 20,000 B.C. Site
of Malta, near Irkutsk, Siberia.
Excavations
by M. M. Gerasimov, 1929.

ally, however, this general principle is disregarded; thus scholars who have made more recent finds, such as those at the Khazar town of Sarkil on the Don (ninth to early twelfth centuries) and at the old Russian town of Staraya Ladoga (thirteenth to fifteenth centuries), store and study their materials in this department.

The archaeological finds in this collection have come to the Hermitage at various times from different organizations engaged in research work in the field. Major contributors have been the Imperial Archaeological Commission, set up in 1859; the Archaeological Institute of the Academy of Sciences of the U.S.S.R.; and a group of small museums where material happened to be stored. Many collections comprise items found during expeditions organized by the Hermitage alone, or in collaboration with state agencies or various republics such as the Russian Federation, the Ukraine, and Central Asia.

Excavations in Russian territory began as early as the first half of the eighteenth century, when the Petersburg Academy of Sciences dispatched a number of expeditions to Siberia. The leaders of these expeditions reported that the pillaging of ancient tombs for

gold and silver objects had become something of a local industry in Siberia. Even so, these excavations unearthed the gold artifacts sent to Peter the Great in 1715–16, which formed the nucleus of the famous Scythian-Siberian collection that was kept in the czars' so-called Kunstkammer from 1762 to 1859 and was subsequently transferred to the Hermitage.

The ancient objects hidden in the barrows on the steppes north of the Black Sea did not claim the attention of scholars until a number of years later. In 1763 an early Scythian barrow (late seventh to early sixth centuries B.C.) was opened up by order of General A. Melgunov. Situated near Elisavetograd (modern

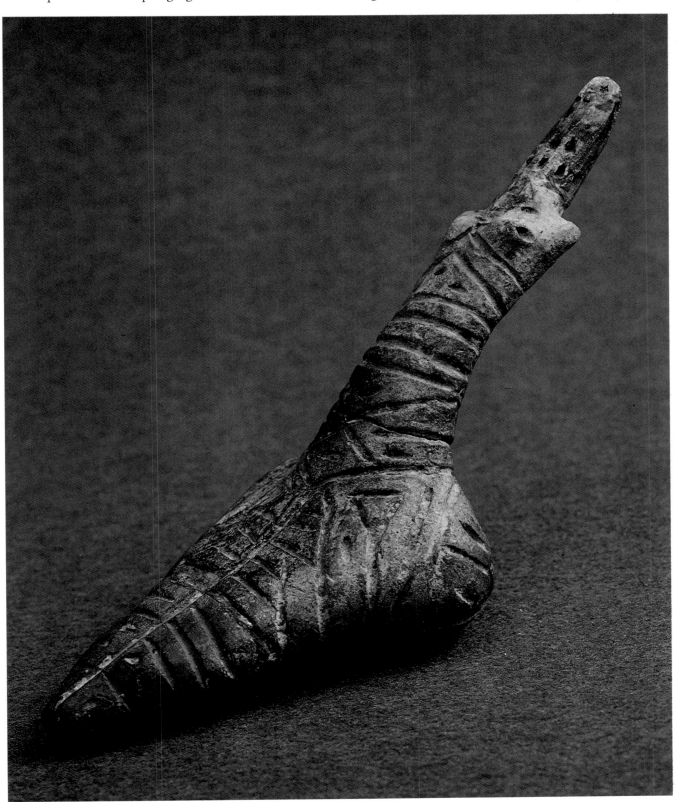

Seated woman.
Terra cotta. Height 12 cm.
First half of third millennium B.C.
Settlement of Bernova-Luka in the
Chernovitsky Oblast, Ukraine.
Excavations by T. S. Passek, 1951.

Kirovograd) in the Ukraine, it proved rich in treasures that subsequently reached the Hermitage by way of the Kunstkammer.

Systematic excavation of the barrows and other tombs of the Scythian kingdom and the kingdom of Bosporus (Crimea and northern Caucasus) began in 1830 with the Kul Oba barrow in the vicinity of Kerch. From that time on it was decreed that all gold objects found were to be sent by way of the Archaeological Commission to the Hermitage, where they came to form the celebrated collections of Scythian gold.

For both storage and exhibition the material is

Vessel with painted ornament.
Terra cotta. Height 17 cm,
maximum diam. 22.7 cm.
Tripolje culture, second half of
third millennium B.C.
Settlement near the village of
Nezvisko, Ukraine.
Excavations by Ye. K. Chernysh,
1953–54.

divided into five major periods: the Paleolithic or Old Stone Age, the Neolithic or New Stone Age, the Aeneolithic or Copper-Stone Age, the Bronze Age, and the Iron Age.

The Paleolithic or Old Stone Age lasted several hundred thousand years, for at that primitive stage humanity's productive forces developed very slowly, requiring a long time to emerge from dependence on nature and the elements in the struggle for survival. The culture of the Old Stone Age, roughly 400,000 years ago, is represented in the Hermitage by rudimentary stone tools found in Armenia at Satani-Dar, on the slopes of Mount Aragats. The principal tools are large stone axes and crudely cut stones with one sharp edge that served various purposes.

The material found at the village of Malta, near Irkutsk in Siberia, belongs to the Upper Paleolithic Period, the second phase of the Old Stone Age. The cult of woman as childbearer and keeper of the hearth, and the cult of animals, played a basic role in the art of the time and had religious and magical significance. These two aspects of primitive art are clearly shown in the finds made at Malta during 1929–30. The female statuettes of mammoth ivory are highly stylized, indicating that this form of art already had a long history. The extremely stylized figurines of birds are very beautiful. There are also images of mammoths and snakes incised in bone, which archaeologists assign to a period some twenty thousand years ago.

During the Neolithic or New Stone Age, which developed at different times in different parts of the world, humanity made considerable progress. The main occupations at that time were still hunting and fishing, but there was progress in agriculture and the rearing of cattle. A large collection of Neolithic objects dating from the second century B.C., found in a peat bog at Shigirski in Siberia (excavations of 1910–14), includes wooden oars, sledge runners, bone arrowheads and fishhooks, stone tools, and a particularly beautiful example of early art: the head of a female elk incised in horn. During the 1966 excavations among the pile dwellings of Usvyaty IV in the region of Pskov, a Hermitage expedition found the figure of a man cut in elk horn. In spite of its stylization, this work is full of feeling and movement.

The rock carvings found over a wide area of the North also belong to the Neolithic Age. The Hermitage possesses a huge slab removed from a cliff on the shores of Lake Onega (Besov Nos or "Devil's Nose"), with carvings of hunting scenes, elks, swans, boats, and magic symbols all shown in silhouette. In 1935 this enormous piece of rock, dating from the mid-third to the early second millennium B.C., was brought by barge from Lake Onega to the Neva River and then directly upriver to the Hermitage.

The spread of human culture was an uneven process. In a favorable climate it advanced more rapidly, and more progressive forms of economy developed. Hunting gradually gave way to farming, and man passed from mere exploitation of natural resources to production in the proper sense of the word. While in the North a Neolithic culture still prevailed, on the steppes and in the forests of the Ukraine a primitive agricultural way of life already existed between the third and early second millennia B.C., to the west of the Dnieper and in Moldavia. This culture is known as the Tripolje culture, after the place where the first relics were found.

In addition to objects made of stone, bone, and clay, at this point we begin to find a number of objects in copper. Of particular interest are the painted clay vessels and the many clay figurines of women and animals. The pots come in a great variety

of graceful, whimsical shapes, and are often entirely covered with designs in white, brown, or black on reddish or yellow backgrounds. These designs are often spirals or concentric circles, but some are formed of unusual patterns of stylized figures of humans and animals. It is not easy to decipher the meaning of these paintings, though they are apparently related to symbols of fertility and the sun cult. The female statuettes are doubtless linked with the cult of fecundity and motherhood. They are elaborately painted or carved, and some of them have been found to contain seeds, confirming the theory that they were fertility amulets. The figures of domestic animals had the par-

Female head.
Terra cotta. Height 5.3 cm.
Tripolje culture, second half of third millennium B.C. Settlement of Krinichki, Odessa Oblast, Ukraine. Excavations by S. S. Gamchenko, 1909.

allel function of magically increasing the numbers of the herd.

Relics similar to those of the Aeneolithic culture of the Ukraine have also been discovered in Turkmenia, where excavations of ancient villages have brought to light a thriving Aeneolithic culture of the third millennium B.C., the typical products of which were painted pots and figurines of humans and animals. The Hermitage has a large collection of objects from these digs, which in cultural development can be compared with those of the Tripolje culture, though there is no direct link between them.

An interesting collection of items dating from the second half of the third millennium B.C. was unearthed from a barrow near Maikop in the northern Caucasus

Female statuette.
Terra cotta. Height 28 cm.
Tripolje culture, second half of third millennium B.C. Settlement of Krinichki, Odessa Oblast, Ukraine. Excavations by S.S Gamchenko, 1909.

Vessel with painted ornament.
Terra cotta. Height 28.8 cm, maximum diam. 26.8 cm.
Tripolje culture, second half of third millennium B.C.
Settlement near the village of Nezvisko, Ukraine.
Excavations by Ye. K. Chernysh, 1953–54.

Figurine of bull.
Decoration of canopy support.
Gold. Height 6 cm.
Middle of third millennium B.C.
Maikop barrow, northern Caucasus.
Excavations by N. I. Veselovsky, 1897.

Vessel engraved with
pictures of animals.
Silver. Height 9.6 cm.
Middle of third millennium B.C.
Maikop barrow, northern Caucasus.
Excavations by N. I. Veselovsky, 1897.

in 1897. Inside a burial mound was a large wooden chamber containing a corpse and the skeletons of two slaves entombed with their master. Two gold vessels and fourteen silver ones were found in the tomb. One of the silver vessels depicts animals near a river, and a mountain landscape. The body was covered by a kind of canopy adorned with gold plaques in the form of lions and bulls, as well as with gold sequins. The hollow poles supporting the canopy had handles of gold and silver in the shape of long-horned bulls. The main tomb was found to contain a diadem of golden rosettes and several strings of gold, silver, carnelian, and turquoise beads. These elaborate objects surely

came from elsewhere, for the nomadic tribes of the northern Caucasus lived on the borders of the ancient Middle Eastern states, to which they supplied cattle; in exchange, the tribal chieftains acquired precious objects such as those in the Maikop barrow. In addition to copper weapons, several knife blades or harpoon heads of flint were discovered. The pottery found was of an equally primitive type belonging to the local northern Caucasian culture.

As techniques advanced, the production of metal objects and weapons took on great importance. Copper objects, however, were not strong enough, and often inferior to their stone equivalents. It was therefore a great technical breakthrough when copper was first mixed with other elements to form alloys, first with arsenic and later, as trade relations expanded, with tin. In this way bronze objects came into being, greatly encouraging intertribal relations, since these new techniques required metals mined in various areas.

The Hermitage collection includes numerous Bronze Age objects found within the Soviet Union. Bronze Age culture was by no means the same all over; it included many different centers revealing quite different relationships between agriculture and cattle breeding, and a division of labor that varied according to the prevailing geographical conditions. The tribes that produced a larger economic surplus out of cattle breeding naturally made this their main occupation, exchanging their surplus for other goods. The culture of the steppes during the Bronze Age has been carefully studied and is represented in the Hermitage by a small number of objects of artistic value. At this time the painting of pottery was replaced by techniques of carv-

Incense burner.
Terra cotta. Height 10 cm.
Catacomb culture, first half of second millennium B.C. Manych.
Excavations by M.I. Artamonov, 1935.

Terra-cotta vessel with ornamentation.
Catacomb culture, second half of second millennium B.C.

Vessel.
Terra cotta. Height 11 cm.
Wooden tomb culture, second half of second millennium B.C. Village of Khryashchevka, Kuibyshev Oblast.
Excavations by N. Ya. Merpert, 1950–52.

ing or pressing the clay. Some of the designs thus obtained were very complex.

Among the cultures of the last phase of the Bronze Age, special mention should be made of the so-called Koban culture that emerged in the Caucasus at the beginning of the first millennium B.C. The first relics of this culture were discovered near the North Ossetian village of Koban in 1868. Excavations and research carried out at other burial places belonging to this culture have provided a wealth of information on ancient metallurgy, which had evolved into a high form of craftsmanship. Particularly beautiful are the bronze battle axes decorated with engravings of animals (deer,

The culture of the Scythians, the first evidence of which came to light on the steppes and in the forests along the northern coast of the Black Sea, belongs to the Iron Age. The Greek historian Herodotus, often called the "father of history," visited the territory of the Scythians about 450 B.C. and left a detailed account of the life of these tribes. The Scythians were divided into tribes having their own names and modes of production. Some tribes—the so-called plowmen Scythians—were engaged in farming, but the great majority were herdsmen.

Herodotus wrote: "The Scythians have no towns or fortifications, and they carry their households with

Fibula in the form of an ax, adorned with dogs attacking a deer. Detail. Bronze. Koban culture, early first millennium B.C. Burial ground near the village of Upper Koban, North Ossetia. Acquired from the Archaeological Commission, 1889; formerly in the K. I. Olshevsky collection.

snakes, and in one case a dog); belt buckles often in the shape of animals such as galloping horses; plaques in the form of rams' heads with forked horns; personal ornaments; trappings for harnesses; and so on. The Hermitage possesses the finest collection of articles from the Koban culture and many other similar objects from the Volga region and Siberia.

them. They are all mounted archers . . . and live in covered wagons." The image of the barbarous Scythians deeply impressed the Greeks, for the Scythians were a strong people who drank their wine undiluted, were masterful archers, owned enormous herds of horses and cattle, and were constantly on the move from place to place.

At the end of the seventh and the beginning of the sixth centuries B.C., a number of Greek colonies were founded on the northern shores of the Black Sea. By way of these colonies the Greeks obtained cattle and grain from the Scythians, but not until the fifth and fourth centuries did contacts between the two peoples become particularly close. Indeed, during this period Greek objects of gold and silver began to be decorated by detailed figures of Scythians with their characteristic clothes, headdresses, and weapons.

Herodotus tells us that the territory of the Scythians had formerly been occupied by the Cimmerians, whom they expelled. Archaeologists have established

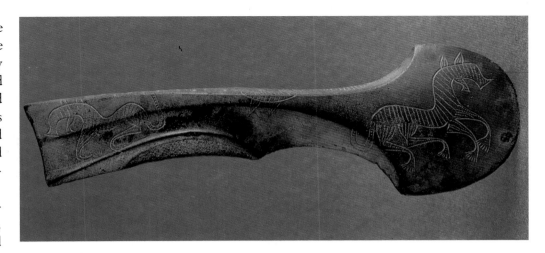

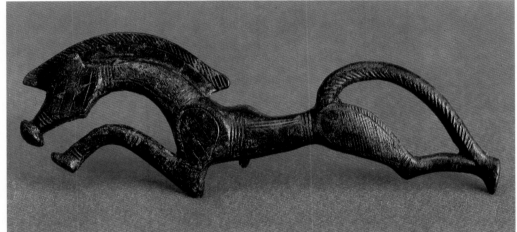

Buckle.
Bronze, inlaid with iron.
Length 24.1 cm.
Koban culture, early first millennium B.C. Burial ground near the village of Upper Koban, North Ossetia.
From the Russian State Museum, 1953.

Ax.
Bronze. Length 16.3 cm.
Eighth to seventh centuries B.C.
Village of Anukhve, Abkhazia.
Found in 1976.

Buckle in the form of a horse.
Bronze. Length 12.9 cm.
Koban culture, first half of first millennium B.C. North Ossetia.
Acquired from the Archaeological Commission, 1889; formerly in the K.I. Olshevsky collection.

Plaque in the form of a panther.
Gold. Length 32.6 cm,
width 16.2 cm.
Early sixth century B.C.
Barrow 1 near the village of
Kelermes, northern Caucasus.
Excavations by D. G. Shults, 1903.

Plaque in the form of a stag.
Gold. Length 31.5 cm,
width 22.5 cm.
Early sixth century B.C.
Barrow near the village of
Kostromskaya, Kuban Area.
Excavations by N. I. Veselovsky, 1897.

Herodotus's claim that the Scythians invaded the countries of the ancient East.

Excavations in the area of the Dnieper have brought to light some early Scythian artifacts (late seventh century B.C.), but most of the Scythian antiquities in the Hermitage date from the sixth to third centuries. The barrows in which the most precious works of art have been found are imposing structures covered with earthworks sometimes as much as twenty meters high. Large numbers of horses were buried along with the tribal chief—as many as 360 have been found in one barrow. The Scythians had close relations with neighboring countries; not only

that the Cimmerian and early Scythian cultures were formed as a synthesis of local and foreign tribes within the general context of Bronze Age culture. In the mid-eighth century B.C., before the Greek colonization of the Black Sea coast, the Cimmerians and then the Scythians raided the neighboring countries of Central Asia; their tribal names have in fact been found in the written records of Assyria and Urartu, confirming

Scythian works of art but also Greek and Oriental objects have been found in these tombs.

Artifacts typical of the Scythian culture include the short iron sword known as the *akinak*; triple-faceted bronze arrowheads with two prongs; a harness with buckles in the form of griffins or rams; and many varied objects decorated with figures of animals often shown fighting one another, such as wild beasts attacking horses or goats. Favorite decorative motifs for Scythian weapons were panthers and couchant stags. Fine examples of large gold plaques in the shape of stags and panthers were found in the excavations at Kostromskaya and Kelermes in the Kuban area.

Ancient Oriental artifacts, especially Urartian and Persian, have also been found in Scythian barrows. Indeed, certain Scythian works of art such as the gold scabbard facings from the barrows at Melgunov and Kelermes, show traces of Urartian influence. They have unusual ornamental motifs and depict—rather inaccurately—scenes of the worship of the sacred tree. Among the Greek objects found in Scythian tombs of the fifth to fourth centuries B.C. are a silver amphora from the Chertomlyk burial mound in the Ukraine excavated in 1863, which shows Scythians breaking in young horses, and a golden comb from the Solokha barrow excavated in 1913, which depicts two Scythian foot soldiers fighting an armored horseman.

A vessel made of electrum (an alloy of gold and silver) found in the Kul Oba barrow in 1830 shows scenes from the mythical account of the origin of the Scythian empire, as narrated by Herodotus. According to this story Targitaos (the Scythian equivalent of Hercules) lost his herd of horses, then found it in the cave of a goddess who was half woman and half ser-

Comb.
Gold. Height 12.3 cm,
width 10.2 cm.
Late fifth to early fourth
centuries B.C. Solokha barrow
near Nikopol, Dnieper Area.
Excavations by N. I. Veselovsky, 1913.

59

Iron sword in scabbard.
Hilt and scabbard faced with gold
leaf bearing pictures in relief.
Length of hilt 15.5 cm,
length of scabbard 47 cm.
Early sixth century B.C.
Barrow 1 near the village of
Kelermes, northern Caucasus.
Excavations by D. G. Shults, 1903.

Ornamental figure of
a mountain goat.
Bronze. Height 18.8 cm.
Tagar culture, sixth to fifth
centuries B.C. Krasnoyarsk Area.
Found by chance, purchased by
G. F. Miller in 1735; transferred
from the Kunstkammer, 1859.

pent. She gave him back his horses in return for his love. According to a prophecy, one of the three sons born of their union—the one who could draw the bow that their father had bequeathed them—was destined to become king of the Scythians. The first two brothers failed in the attempt, but the third, whose name was Scyth, was successful. The Kul Oba vessel shows the two brothers who failed, one injured in the cheekbone and the other in the leg, and the third in his moment of triumph.

In early days archaeologists studied Scythian culture only around the Black Sea, but as research expanded, the known area of Scythian culture grew. It was discovered that the culture of the Sarmatians, who were related to the Scythians, flourished farther to the east across the Don, in the Volga region and in the southern Urals. Indeed, remains of Scythian culture have been found and studied still farther to the east. In a barrow in the Chiliktin Valley of eastern Kazakhstan, thieves who looted the tomb in ancient times left behind the remnants of a wooden quiver with bronze arrowheads of the Scythian type. Discovered during the excavations of 1960, this quiver was decorated with gold plates shaped like couchant deer.

Even farther to the east, in 1929 several barrows made for chiefs of cattle-breeding tribes (fifth to fourth centuries B.C.) were found in the Altai Mountains at 1,500–1,600 meters above sea level. Situated in the Pazyryk Valley, these tombs were unusually well preserved because a layer of permafrost had formed under them almost immediately after the burial, thus protecting about five thousand articles of wood, cloth, felt, leather, and fur—materials rarely spared by the ravages of time. Though this vast collection re-

Ornamental figure of a griffin
with a deer head in its beak.
Wood, leather. Height 27 cm.
Fifth to fourth centuries B.C.
Pazyryk tomb 2, eastern Altai.
Excavations by S. I. Rudenko, 1947.

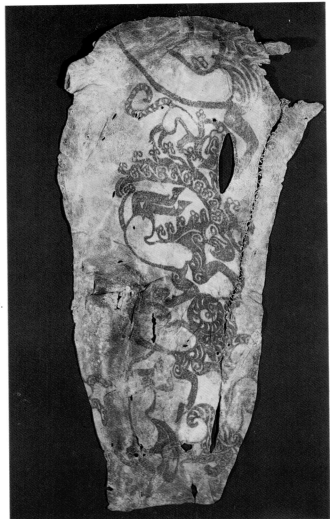

quired extensive restoration, it is one of the most impressive and significant in the Hermitage. The body of a chief was placed in a coffin made of a hollowed-out tree trunk, which in turn was enclosed in a framework of solid logs. The corpse had been embalmed prior to burial; still visible on the skin are tattoos of animals, fish, and mythical creatures. The chief's wife was buried with him, as were clothes, ornaments, everyday implements, musical instruments—in short, all the objects that had surrounded him in life.

By the outer wall of the burial chamber a number of funeral objects were found, including a wooden chariot with high wheels, a large felt carpet, and the remains of slaughtered horses. The latter were complete with saddles and bridles adorned with plaques in the form of animals: birds and mythical creatures carved out of wood and partly covered with gold leaf. The horses' heads were covered with masks, of which two are particularly interesting: one in the shape of a stag's head with branching antlers, and the other resembling a griffin.

Perhaps the most extraordinary finds in the Pazyryk barrows were a woolen pile carpet of Persian workmanship that is the oldest carpet known to us; Achaemenian silks from Persia; and a piece of Chinese silk dating from the fifth century B.C.—also the oldest

of its kind ever discovered. The representations of animals in the Pazyryk finds are indeed very close in style to Scythian work.

Such, in brief, was the discovery of the Scythian world, until recently unknown or forgotten, though it preceded the more southerly Silk Route in forming a bridge between Eastern Europe and the Far East.

Many cultural elements were common to the vast area between the Danube in the west and the Ordos region in the east. This area formed a broad band of steppes, foothills, and mountains more than seven thousand kilometers long between the fortieth and fiftieth parallels. Throughout this territory we can see the same weapons, the same harnesses, and a common art—the so-called Animal Style, characterized by expressive scenes of wild beasts fighting. All the nomadic tribes of herdsmen reveal an identical level of development, and an economy primarily based on horse breeding. The network of relationships among these tribes made up for the lack of natural resources in certain areas, and especially for the shortage of metals. While contacts between distant peoples in the Mediterranean were maintained by seafarers, here they were assured by mounted couriers. Squadrons of well-armed horsemen were likewise capable of covering vast distances at great speed.

Also related to this group of archaeological discoveries is the collection of works of the Tagar culture, which flourished in the Minusinsk region during the seventh to eighth centuries A.D. The bronze daggers, sheaths with figures of mountain goats, and large bronze cauldrons all resemble Scythian wares.

Siberia has provided the Hermitage with yet another series of ancient objects in an incredibly good state of preservation. In 1969 a burial mound of the Tashtyk culture (first century B.C.) was excavated at Oglakhty, in the middle of the Yenisei River basin. Wooden burial chambers contained the remains of several bodies dressed in furs, thin faces covered with painted plaster masks.

During the third century B.C. the Sarmatian tribes began pushing westward toward the steppes north of the Black Sea, forcing out the Scythians and spreading their own culture. The Novocherkassk Treasure, discovered near the town of that name in 1864 (also known as the Circassian Treasure), is one of the most outstanding examples of Sarmatian culture between the first century B.C. and the first century A.D. Found in a tomb, the collection consists of gold ornaments, diadems, and vessels of various kinds distinguished by their intricate forms and the complexity of their decoration, most of it depicting imaginary animals. The jewelry of this period was lavishly inlaid with precious stones, glass, and pearls.

In the fourth century A.D. Sarmatian culture came to an end, giving way to the age of great migrations. The Huns became the masters of the steppes. The cul-

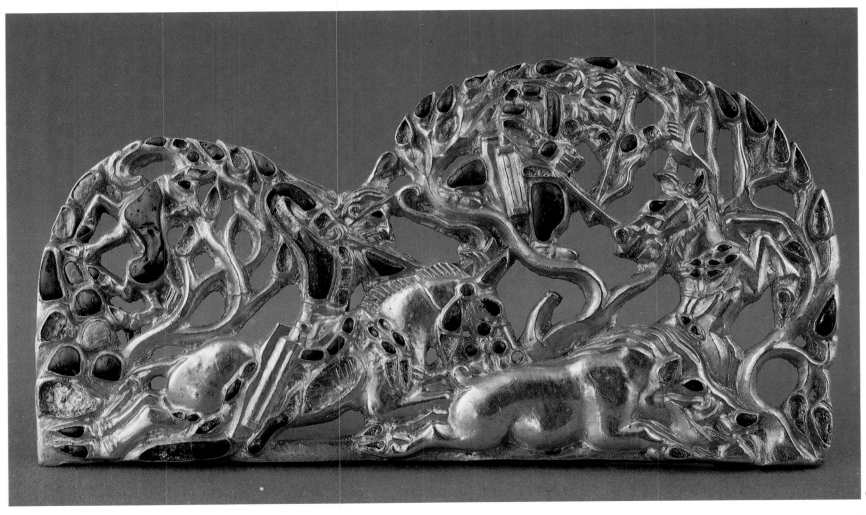

ture of the early Middle Ages, of the Alani and the Goths who settled in the Crimea, is represented by materials from the Suuk-Su excavations. Dating from the sixth and seventh centuries A.D., these objects reveal the strong influence of Byzantine culture.

The great collection of gold and silver objects found in 1912 in the village of Malaya Pereshchepina, near Poltava, dates from the late seventh century. Consisting of about twenty-five kilos of gold and fifty of silver, it includes objects of various origins. The earliest item is a Sassanian dish of the first half of the fourth century. Made in the Persian style, it bears a portrait of King Shapur II. The Byzantine objects,

and in particular the dish of Bishop Paternus, date from the sixth century. Though it has been established when this treasure was assembled from the dates on the Byzantine coins it contains (602–688 A.D.), it is hard to say whether it was plundered treasure or riches accumulated by the chief of one of the nomadic tribes of the steppes and buried along with him.

The remaining collections in this department include Slavic and Old Russian antiquities of the sixth to thirteenth centuries, found in various regions of the country. As excavations continue, the department is constantly being enlarged by new finds.

Vase.
Electrum (alloy of gold and silver).
Height 13 cm.
Late fifth to early fourth
centuries B.C. Kul Oba
(ash mound) barrow near Kerch.
Found by chance, 1830.

Vase.
Gilded silver. Height 70 cm.
First half of fourth century B.C.
Chertomlyk burial mound near
Nikopol, Dnieper Area.
Excavations by I. Ye. Zabelin, 1863.

The Department of Antiquities

When the New Hermitage was opened in February 1852, the museum consisted of only two departments. One of these, with a staff of eight, included the library and collections of engravings, coins and medals, glyptics, and classical vases and assorted objects. It occupied the ground floor of the new building, and nine of its eighteen exhibition halls were devoted to antiquities. The first exhibition, which brought together the works of antiquity in Petersburg and its environs as well as some recent acquisitions, was the nucleus from which the Antiquities Department was later formed.

The first works of ancient art were seen in Russia

Ionian-Rhodian vase.
Terra cotta. Height 27 cm.
C. 640 B.C. Found in the
Temir-gora barrow, Kerch, in 1870.

Pythos, showing
Oriental influence in style.
Terra cotta. Height 84.8 cm.
Etruria, late seventh to early
sixth century B.C.
Acquired with the
Campana collection, 1862.

long before the museum was founded. While in charge of a group of Russian painters studying in Italy, Yuri Kologrivov, on orders from Peter the Great, bought a statue of Venus that was in fact a Roman copy of a third-century B.C. Greek original. This statue had been discovered in 1718, and Governor Falconieri refused to allow its removal from Rome, much to the despair of Kologrivov. The czar then instructed his envoy, Savva Raguzinsky, to offer the relics of St. Bridget in exchange for the pagan statue, and Pope Clement XI was forced to accept. After its long journey to Petersburg the Venus was at first installed in the Summer Garden and then in the

Tauride Palace, becoming known as the *Tauride Venus*. From this palace it was finally brought to the Hermitage and set up in the hall where it stands to this day. Peter the Great also bought other statues, including one of an old shepherd (second century B.C.) carrying two partridges in a bag and a kid in his right hand. In 1851, before the New Hermitage was opened, Pope Pius IX sent seven pieces of sculpture from Rome, including a *Satyr* and *Eros Stringing His Bow*, in exchange for a plot of land on the Palatine that belonged to the Russian government.

Among the classical works that came to the Hermitage before the mid-nineteenth century, special mention should be made of the Lyde Brown collection, which was bought in 1787. It includes a fine bust of the Roman emperor Philip the Arabian. The statues from this collection were originally housed at Tsarskoe Selo, at Pavlovsk, and in the Tauride Garden, but in the mid-nineteenth century they were transferred to the Antiquities Department, which had just been established in the Hermitage. This collection

was then supplemented by a number of ancient statues owned by the Demidov family, among them *Athena* and *Resting Satyr*, as well as forty-six items belonging to Ivan Laval, including a portrait of Emperor Balbinus. The Hermitage collection of antique painted vases, terra cottas, and small bronzes began in 1834, when the Pizzati collection was purchased in Rome. Part of this was distributed among other museums but later reassembled at the Hermitage.

Since its founding, the Antiquities Department has been continually enlarged by the purchase of single objects and by collections such as those of Saburov, Shuvalov, Botkin, and Tolstoy. But the most impor-

Euphronios.
Red-figure psykter:
hetaerae feasting.
Terra cotta. Height 34 cm.
Attica, 505–500 B.C.
Acquired with the
Campana collection, 1862.

Vessel in the form of a sphinx.
Terra cotta. Height 21.5 cm.
Attica, late fifth century B.C.
From the Sennaya necropolis,
ancient Phanagoria, Taman Peninsula.

67

tant single purchase of classical antiquities for the Hermitage was made by Stepan Gedeonov at an auction in Rome in 1861–62. This included 787 items of the collection of the Marchese Campana, among which were numerous painted pots, bronze articles, and sculpture. The 3.47-meter-high statue of Jupiter seated on his throne—the largest statue in the Hermitage—came from this collection, as did the statue of Athena known as the *Athena Campana*. Many of the items purchased had been considerably restored, with statues composed of parts from different pieces, while the pottery had been put together according to the methods of the time. Needless to say, it took endless care and labor to sort out the authentic parts from the additions and to assign parts of the composite pieces to the right originals.

In the 1830s archaeological research in the south of Russia began to open up a new world: ancient Greek colonies and ancient states such as the kingdom of Bosporus. A Greek colony had been established on the island of Berezan in the late seventh century B.C., while at the beginning of the sixth century B.C. colonists from Miletus founded the city of Olbia near the mouth of the Bug. In the first half of the sixth century B.C. the Ionian colonies of Panticapaeum, Phanagoris, and Nymphaeum were established, and Chersonesus only a little later.

Excavation of these sites, initiated by the Imperial Archaeological Commission with the assistance of local cultural institutes, uncovered a wealth of material, the best of which went to the Hermitage. Studies of these colonies on the north coast of the Black Sea are still proceeding, with appreciable results. At Berezan, Olbia, Nymphaeum, and Chersonesus the work is carried out by expeditions from the Hermitage; every year adds new items to the museum's collection.

Excavations at the cities mentioned have furnished the museum with some first-class works of art, jewelry in particular. The Scythian barrows of the fifth to third centuries B.C. contained pieces of ancient Greek art acquired by the Scythians through trade, some of them made by the Greeks specifically for the Scythians. These were decorated with scenes of nomadic life on the steppes north of the Black Sea or with episodes from myths and legends that we know of from Herodotus.

The excavation of the Kul Oba barrow near Kerch, carried out in September 1830, was the first important step in the study of these ancient remains. Even though thieves at one point broke in and stole many of the precious finds, not all of which were recovered, this barrow provided archaeologists with an enormous quantity of material, including many gold objects of Greek manufacture such as an electrum vessel with the figures of Scythians, pendants representing the head of Athena, a golden phial, a figurine of a stag designed as an ornament for a shield, and a necklace decorated with small figures of Scythian horsemen.

In February 1831 these valuable items were taken to the Winter Palace in Petersburg, prompting the Court Ministry to allocate considerable funds for further research. This in turn led to the establishment of the Hall of Kerch Antiquities in the New Hermitage, containing more than seventeen hundred items. The most precious gold artifacts were at first given a place of honor in a small second-floor room known as the Empress's Study, subsequently occupied by frescoes of the school of Raphael brought from a villa on the Palatine Hill in Rome. We can get a general idea of how this room looked from a watercolor by Eduard Gau dating from 1856. In an account of the Hermitage as it was in 1861, this room is described as being "full of the most extraordinary golden objects from Kerch to be found anywhere in Europe." Along with Scythian treasures that came to the Hermitage much later, these priceless pieces are now kept in the Special Storeroom.

The greater part of the classical sculpture in this department was bought in Italy; for this reason the Hermitage is particularly rich in Roman statues, many of which are copies of Greek originals of the fifth to third centuries B.C. Though bearing some imprint of the time in which they were made, these copies convey an eloquent notion of Greek sculpture in its prime. The statue of Asclepius from Ostia and the head of the *Discobolus* are copies of originals by Myron; the *Athena Campana* is clearly inspired by the school of Phidias himself; and the dark basalt head of the *Doryphoros* is a reproduction of a statue by Polykleitus well known in antiquity.

With equal effectiveness, Roman sculpture echoes works of the great Greek masters of the fourth century B.C. Thus the influence of Scopas is evident in the figure of Hercules holding a lion's skin and an apple; the *Resting Satyr* from the Demidov collection reproduces one of the most celebrated works of Praxiteles; and the small group of marble sculptures known as *Hercules Slaying the Nemean Lion* is a copy of a bronze by Lysippus. The *Tauride Venus* mentioned above is a brilliant first-century A.D. copy of a third-century B.C. Hellenic statue. Original Greek works in the Hermitage come from excavations of ancient Greek cities on the north coast of the Black Sea. Worthy of mention are the statue of Cybele (fifth century B.C.) and that of a king of Bosporus (fourth century B.C.), both found at Panticapaeum in the region of Kerch.

Large-scale Greek sculpture is reproduced in miniature in small bronzes such as the statuette of Poseidon (fifth century B.C.) and that of a seated youth playing the cithara (third century B.C.), which suggest the influence of the great fifth-century sculptor Pythagoras of Rhegium. The collection of Greek bronzes is

1. Euphronios (?).
Red-figure pelike:
the first swallow.
Terra cotta. Height 37.5 cm.
Attica, late sixth century B.C.
Acquired with the Abaza collection,
1901.

2. Nikosthenes.
Red-figure kantharos: six youths
dancing and playing instruments.
Terra cotta. Height 23.5 cm.
Attica, 520 B.C.
Transferred from the Stieglitz
Museum in 1926. Presented by
Heinrich Schliemann to Alexander
Stieglitz in 1886.

3. The Amasis painter.
Black-figure amphora:
rider and warriors.
Terra cotta. Height 31 cm.
Attica. 540 B.C.
Acquired with the Pizzati
collection, 1834.

4. Skythes.
Black-figure hydria:
nuptial chariot.
Terra cotta. Height 32 cm.
Attica, c. 520 B.C.
Acquired with the Abaza collection,
1901.

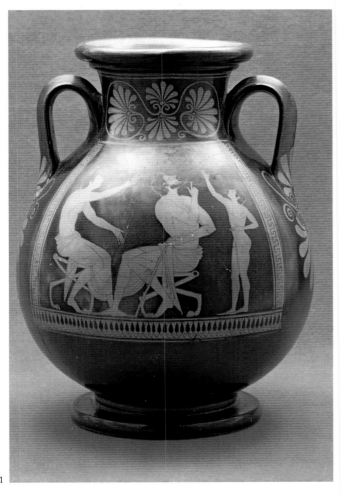

1

2

3

4

69

Dexamenos of Chios.
Seal: the Flying Heron.
Chalcedony and gold. 2.2 × 1.7 cm.
Greece, fifth century B.C.
Found in the Panticapaeum
necropolis, Kerch. In the
Hermitage since 1860.

The Gonzaga Cameo:
Ptolemy II and his wife Arsinoë.
Sardonyx. 15.7 × 11.8 cm.
Alexandria, third century B.C.
Given to Alexander I
by the ex-Empress Josephine in 1814.

Cameo: Tiberius.
Sardonyx. 2.5 × 2.1 cm.
Rome, early first century A.D.
Acquired from the Duke of
Saint Moritz collection, 1792.

extremely varied. Representing the sixth century B.C. are figurines of young men (*kouroi*) connected with ancient funerary rites. The subsequent period is represented by statuettes of warriors with spear and shield, and male and female figures. The Hermitage also possesses some fine Etruscan and Italic bronzes: votive figures of gods, priests, people, and animals. Two items deserve special mention: a bronze lion of the early fifth century B.C. with its fangs bared and its body tensed to spring, and a large (42-centimeter-high) mid-fourth-century B.C. bronze cinerary urn in the form of a reclining youth. Both these pieces come from the Campana collection.

The Roman portrait sculpture—of fundamental importance in the evolution of Western European sculpture, especially during the Renaissance—constitutes the most valuable and interesting collection in the department, and enables us to follow the evolution of this art from the first century B.C. to the fourth century A.D. The Hermitage collection was formed over a long span of time. The first works of portrait sculpture were purchased by Catherine the Great in the 1760s, but perhaps the most important acquisition was the purchase in 1784–87 of the Lyde Brown collection, which included the finest work of its kind. The buying of Roman sculpture, however, continued until the 1930s.

Among the most ancient pieces is an exceptionally fine bronze head of an unknown Roman (first century B.C.), remarkable for its realism and individuality. The statues and busts of Roman emperors, however, were conceived and executed with a quite different purpose in mind, and were set up in all the public places and buildings of ancient Rome. Such was their quantity that in the sixth century Cassiodorus wrote: "Within the walls of Rome there dwells another people: the statues." According to some estimates there were no fewer than 3,785 of these works throughout the city. The Campana collection gave the museum a marble statue of Augustus represented as Jupiter seated on a throne, in one hand a scepter and in the other an orb bearing the image of Nike, goddess of victory. It is a highly idealized portrait intended to exalt the emperor after his death. The portrait of his wife, Livia, in the guise of Ceres-Augusta, first priestess of the cult of Augustus, is likewise extremely idealized.

The marble busts of the second century A.D., such as that of Lucius Verus and the *Syrian Woman*, are entirely different in style and purpose: here the artist has attempted not only to achieve a good likeness but to portray the innate character of his model. This tendency becomes particularly marked in the second quarter of the third century A.D., with the evolution of "psychological" portraits, outstanding as penetrating character studies. The best examples of this kind are the bust of Emperor Balbinus, a man of great culture but little will power, and that of another emperor, Philip the Arabian.

The Antiquities Department also contains Roman sarcophagi of the third century A.D., works of real quality decorated with both high and low reliefs depicting scenes from ancient myths: Hippolytus and Phaedra, the rape of Persephone, Apollo and the

Muses, wedding scenes, and so on. In the wedding scenes the faces of the bride and bridegroom appear to be realistic portraits, while likenesses of the dead were carved on the sides of the sarcophagi, sometimes surrounded by medallions supported by two genii. The museum also has a vast collection of marble and limestone reliefs, funerary stelae, and ethnographic finds, most from the Greek and Roman colonies north of the Black Sea.

The Antiquities Department has a large collection of painted pottery of which the museum is justly proud; including fragments, it numbers over fifteen thousand pieces. They come from collections great

has also had its effect on the department's contents.

The museum possesses good collections of Corinthian ware of the seventh to sixth centuries B.C., black- and red-figure Attic vases of the sixth to fourth centuries B.C. (the most valuable items), Etruscan pottery of the seventh to fifth centuries B.C., and Italic vases mostly from the fourth century B.C. Even in the archaic period (seventh century B.C.) Greece could boast of several major centers producing painted vases: Corinth, the islands of Rhodes and Samos, and a number of other places in Ionia. Each center's style had its own individual characteristics.

The seventh-to-sixth century B.C. vases from Cor-

Cinerary urn: reclining youth.
Bronze. Length of base 69 cm, height 42 cm.
Etruria, mid-fourth century B.C.
Found in Perugia in 1843. Acquired with the Campana collection, 1862.

and small acquired by the museum, from private individuals, and from excavations on the northern Black Sea coast. Pottery obtained directly from excavations is of particular value, as it is found in conjunction with other objects that can be accurately dated, and thereby provides a point of reference for the study and classification of the pottery included in the older collections, which originally reached the museum without any indications of origin.

The collection of ancient pottery is somewhat uneven, as it contains very few examples of archaic work from before the seventh century B.C. In the collections bought in the first half of the nineteenth century these are lacking altogether, for interest in early history was then in its infancy, while black- and red-figure vases were all the rage with collectors because of the variety of themes used in the painting. The fact that both the main collections (the Pizzati and Campana, bought in 1834 and 1861–62, respectively) were acquired in Italy

inth are distinguished by their exquisite workmanship and the combination of several decorative motifs. Common features are processions of animals in silhouette, with the spaces between them filled by rosettes. The influence of Middle Eastern art is discernible in these. Many of the compositions are heraldic, showing for example a bird between sphinxes, a siren between lions, or a winged youth between panthers.

Noteworthy examples of seventh-to-sixth-century B.C. vases have come to light in the course of excavations north of the Black Sea. For instance, the 1870 excavation of the Temir-gora barrow in Kerch revealed a mid-seventh-century B.C. painted vase with a double row of bulls, gazelles, hares, and dogs in motion. As with Corinthian vases, the spaces between the figures are occupied by complex ornamental motifs such as rosettes, swastikas, and crosses. This particular vase is in the Ionian-Rhodian style. On the island of Berezan, numerous fragments of Samos ware belonging to the mid-sixth century B.C. have been discovered, as well as an almost complete amphora showing two figures drinking wine.

Some of the vases have been attributed to famous painters of antiquity. Three may be reliably ascribed to the celebrated Amasis painter (third quarter of the sixth century B.C.), including an amphora bearing the figures of warriors and horses, painted in his characteristically delicate style and showing Middle Eastern influence. One black-figure hydria depicting the nuptial chariots of Zeus and Hera is the work of the master Skythes.

Some of the black-figure Panathenaic amphoras were found in the Ak-burun and Zelenski barrows north of the Black Sea.

The collection of red-figure vases contains work by other famous painters such as Psiax, Nikosthenes, Euphronios, the Pan painter, and the Kleophon painter. Of the three vases attributed to Euphronios (late sixth century B.C.), two are particularly noteworthy. One is a psykter (a vessel used for cooling wine) decorated with the figures of four banqueting hetaerae, with an indication of their names and the signature the artist. One of them, as she spills some wine from a bowl, says, "I pour this [drop] for you, Leager." The second of these vessels, a pelike, shows the return of spring and the appearance of the first swallow. An old man, a young man, and a boy are shown greeting this event, their dialogue inscribed in Greek above their heads. "Look, a swallow!" says the young man, whereupon the bearded man exclaims, "By Heracles!" and the boy notes joyously, "There she is—spring!" The other side of the same vessel shows two youths wrestling and the inscription, "Leager is a beautiful youth," probably referring to the same young man in whose honor the hetaera on the psykter poured out her drop of wine. This work came to the Hermitage in 1901 from the collection of A. A. Abaza, then finance minister, who had won the vase at cards.

No less curious is the origin of a kantharos attributed to the painter Nikosthenes and said to come from the workshop of Pampheus. The museum acquired it from the collection of Stieglitz, who had received it in 1886 from Heinrich Schliemann. The painting is a complex composition involving several figures. On one side Hercules is wrestling with a lion while Athena, Hermes, Iolaus, and two women watch; on the other side a group of six young men (komasti) are dancing and playing musical instruments.

Deserving special mention also are the vases in the shape of human or animal heads, and in particular a late-fifth-century B.C. Attic vase in the form of a sphinx, found in 1869 at Phanagoria on the Taman Peninsula. This mythical creature with a lion's body, a bird's wings, and the head of a young woman has retained its original paint and gilding and is outstanding

Aphrodite,
the so-called *Tauride Venus.*
Marble. Height 167 cm.
First-century A.D. Roman copy of
a third-century B.C. Greek original.
Found in Rome in 1718.
Presented by Pope Clement XI to
Peter the Great. Transferred from
the Tauride Palace in 1850.

for the delicacy of its workmanship. It ranks among the masterpieces of ancient art.

Italic ceramics are also abundantly represented, including several vases dating from the so-called Villanova culture (eighth century B.C.), which preceded the Etruscans. But the most interesting collection is the Etruscan pottery of the seventh to sixth centuries B.C. Decorated like Corinthian vases with processions of mountain goats, panthers, and lions, austere in style, and executed in brownish-red, the large pithoi are truly monumental in appearance. A second type of Etruscan ceramic work, the so-called bucchero, consists of black vessels with highly glazed surfaces resembling metal. Among the latter is an enormous vessel on a tall stand, decorated with stylized animals and equipped with lion's-head handles, reminiscent of the Urartian bronzes mentioned earlier.

Another Italic vase deserving mention is a late-fourth-century hydria from the necropolis at Cumae (Campana collection), the graceful black-lacquered body of which also resembles metal. It bears two bands of decorative figures in relief, one under the handles, the other just below the neck. The lower band is made up of wild animals and griffins, while the upper one contains figures associated with the Eleusinian mysteries: Demeter with her daughter

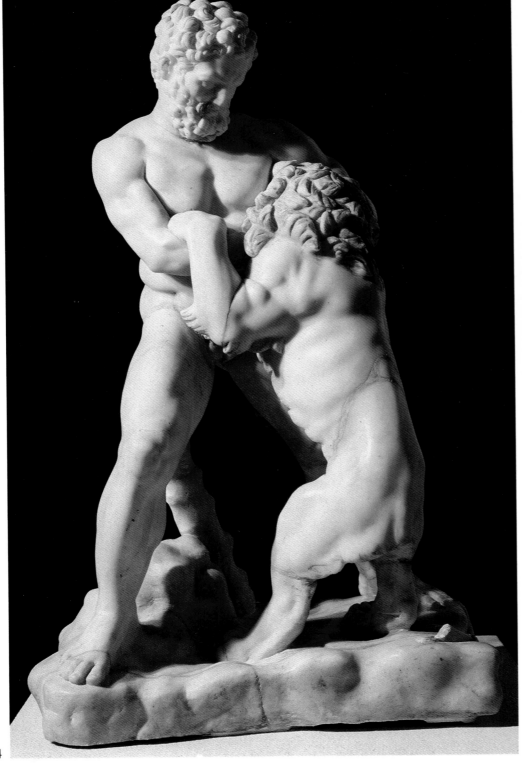

Persephone, Dionysus, Artemis, Aphrodite, Athena, and Eubuleus, the supposed founder of the cult. The figures have retained their white color and gilding, and the vase is rightly called the "Regina Vasorum," Queen of Vases.

We cannot fail to mention the collection of terra cottas from both Greek and Italic centers and from sites north of the Black Sea: Berezan, Olbia, Nymphaeum, and the Bolshaya Bliznitsa barrow on the Taman Peninsula. Visitors to the museum show special interest in the famous terra cottas from Tanagra in Boeotia, dating from the late fourth and third centuries B.C. Most of these came to the museum in 1884 from the collection of P. Saburov. The craftsmen of Tanagra were particularly skillful at creating lifelike statues, chiefly of women, out of a number of separate pieces. To a large extent, these still retain their painting and gilding on a white background. In many of them one can discern the influence of the great Greek masters, such as Praxiteles and Lysippus.

Last but not least is the department's superlative

collection of intaglios and cameos. Already by the end of the eighteenth century this collection comprised over ten thousand items, though at that time no distinction was made between ancient and Western European art. Catherine the Great was a keen collector of carved stones, the first group of which reached the Hermitage in 1764, along with the earliest paintings. Later on, between 1780 and 1792, one purchase of gems followed another, including the collections of Breteuil; Lord Beverley; Louis-Philippe, Duke of Orleans; and G. J. Casanova, then director of the Dresden Academy of Arts.

The collection of carved stones was also enlarged considerably during the nineteenth century. In 1814 the ex-Empress Josephine presented Czar Alexander I with the famous Gonzaga cameo, one of the largest and finest of all ancient glyptics, bearing the figures of Ptolemy II and his wife Arsinoë and dating from the third century B.C. Ownership of the cameo can be traced back to 1542, when it belonged to Duke Gonzaga of Mantua. But in 1630 the Austrians overran Mantua and removed the cameo to Prague. Later it was taken as booty by the invading Swedes and became part of the treasure of Queen Christina of Sweden. Following her abdication the cameo returned to Italy, where by way of the Odescalchi collection it

Hercules Slaying the Nemean Lion.
Marble. Height 65 cm.
Roman copy after Lysippus,
late fourth century B.C.
Acquired from
the Golitsyn collection, 1887.

Head of *Discobolus.*
Marble. Height 28 cm.
Roman copy of a Greek original
by Myron from the second half of
the fifth century B.C.
Acquired before 1859.

Aphrodite and Eros.
Terra cotta. Height 18.5 cm.
Tanagra (Boeotia),
late fourth century B.C.
Acquired with the Saburov collection,
1884.

Standing woman.
Terra cotta. Height 18 cm.
Tanagra (Boeotia),
third century B.C.
Acquired with the Saburov
collection, 1884.

found its way into the Vatican. From there, in 1798, it was taken to France.

The growth of the collection has continued during the nineteenth and twentieth centuries with the acquisition of private collections. But the most valuable source of carved stones has been the archaeological excavations of ancient sites and Scythian barrows north of the Black Sea.

The Hermitage also possesses a small number of seals dating from the Aegean civilization (second millennium B.C.), from the Homeric period (tenth to eighth centuries B.C.), and from archaic Greece (sixth century B.C.), as well as glyptics of the classical Greek period (fifth to fourth centuries B.C.) and the Hellenic age (third to first centuries B.C.).

Among the finest works of the fifth century B.C. are the intaglios of Dexamenos of Chios; the famous work from Panticapaeum (Kerch) depicting a heron in flight and signed by the artist; the galloping horse also from Panticapaeum; and the gold-framed stone depicting a grasshopper, found in the Malaya Bliznitsa barrow on the Taman Peninsula and attributed to a master of the school of Dexamenos. Items from ancient Rome include intaglios and cameo portraits of Caracalla (third century A.D.), Tiberius (early first century), and Livia (late first century).

Portrait of a Roman woman,
the so-called *Syrian Woman*.
Marble. Height 30 cm.
Possibly by a Greek master.
160–170 A.D.
Acquired before 1850.

Portrait of a Roman.
Bronze. Height 39 cm.
Late first century B.C.
In the Hermitage since 1928.

76

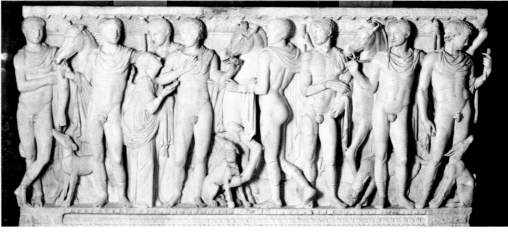

Sarcophagus:
Phaedra and Hippolytus.
Marble. Height 125 cm,
length 230 cm, width 119 cm.
Mid-third century A.D.
Found in the via Aurelia, Rome,
in 1853. Acquired with the
Campana collection, 1862.

Philip the Arabian.
Marble. Height 72.3 cm.
Second quarter of the third
century A.D.
Acquired with the Lyde Brown
collection, 1787.

Augustus as Jupiter.
Marble. Height 185 cm.
First quarter of the first century A.D.
Acquired with the Campana
collection, 1862.

Augustus Room
in the New Hermitage.
Roman art from
the time of the Republic and
the Julio-Claudian Dynasty.

Hercules Room
in the New Hermitage.
Greek sculpture
of the fourth century B.C.

Athena Room in the New Hermitage.
Mosaic floor from a late-antiquity
basilica in Chersonesus.
Excavations by A. F. Uvarov, 1853.

The Department of the History of Oriental Culture

exhibit in 1852 in the New Hermitage, in the specially designed Egyptian Sculpture Room, the general appearance of which has been preserved for us in the watercolors of Konstantin Ukhtomsky. Among the items then on display were numerous small objects from the Alexandra Laval collection; a large granite statue of the lion-headed goddess Sekhmet brought back by the traveler Avraam Norov in 1837, that had long been collecting dust under the stairs at the Academy of Arts; a group sculpture of the high priest Amenemheb with his wife and mother; and two large granite sarcophagi dating from the Twenty-sixth Dynasty, discovered at Giza near the pyramid of

Statue of Amenemhet III,
Twelfth Dynasty.
Porphyry. Height 86.5 cm.
Second half of
nineteenth century B.C.

Statuette of Pharaoh Taharqa.
Bronze. Height 18.5 cm.
Seventh century B.C.

The Oriental Department was established in 1920, while the Hermitage was still awaiting the return of the treasures evacuated to Moscow. On November 18 of that year crates of objects began to arrive at the museum; earlier, on November 1, the Hermitage Council had already decided to set up a Department of the Moslem East, which became the core of the new department. By no means accidental, this decision resulted from a sudden growth in the study of Oriental art, which brought with it a new awareness of the Eastern peoples' contribution to culture as a whole.

By 1920 the Hermitage already possessed examples of Oriental art, particularly Persian, which formed part of the medieval section and were on display in a small ground-floor room of the Felten building. Peter the Great's Kunstkammer also held Oriental objects. Some splendid examples of Oriental applied arts reached the Hermitage by way of Aleksandr Bazilevsky's collection and through the Imperial Archaeological Commission. The Arsenal contained some fine examples of highly decorated weapons, while the Numismatics Department was famed for its collection of Oriental coins.

In 1921 the Department of the Moslem East became the Department of the Caucasus, Iran, and Central Asia, with greatly enlarged activities. At first the department had no permanent display space of its own and could only on occasion mount special exhibitions of particularly interesting items. In 1925 new finds and acquisitions of Oriental art began to arrive at the Hermitage, and at last a permanent exhibition devoted to the Caucasus, Iran, and Central Asia was set up in the Winter Palace, stressing the common features of the Christian and Moslem peoples of the East. Later on, the department was enlarged to include other countries outside the Soviet Union: Egypt, Syria, Turkey, India, China, and Japan. At this point it was divided into four sections: the Ancient East, Middle East and Byzantium, the Far East and India, the Caucasus and Central Asia. Egyptian, Mesopotamian, and Urartian items form the basis of the Ancient East section.

The Egyptian collection, though small, includes a number of celebrated items. They were first put on

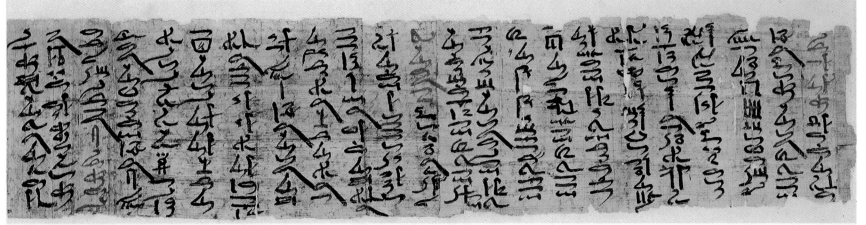

Khafre and presented to the Hermitage by the Duke of Leuchtenberg in 1852.

Elsewhere in Petersburg, in the Kunstkammer of the Academy of Sciences, there was a hall painted in Egyptian style in which a collection called the Egyptian Museum was displayed, built around the Castiglione collection purchased in 1825. The very existence of this collection demonstrates the profound interest that Russian scholars were then taking in the monuments of ancient Egypt and the deciphering of hieroglyphics. It was not by chance that Jean-François Champollion, who discovered the secret of Egyptian writing, was elected a foreign member of the Petersburg Academy of Sciences in 1827.

In 1862, items on exhibit at the Egyptian Museum began their move to the Hermitage, a process that was completed in 1881. The Ancient Egyptian collection, much enlarged, was moved from the small room where it had always been housed to the hall on the right of the lobby inside the caryatid portico. A number of small collections and private purchases were added to it thereafter. Among the Hermitage's possessions is one of the most famous Egyptian literary texts extant, *The Tale of the Shipwrecked Man,* dating from the Middle Kingdom. This papyrus tells the story of an Egyptian cast up on a desert island when his ship sank on its way to the southerly land of Punt, and how he was saved by the dragon who ruled the island.

Other renowned holdings are the statue of Amenemhet III of the Twelfth Dynasty; the stone stela of the future pharaoh Horemheb, founder of the Nineteenth Dynasty; and a small bronze statue of Taharqa, a member of the Twenty-fifth Dynasty of the Nubian pharaohs.

The museum also possesses relics of the First to Twelfth Dynasties found during the 1961–63 Nubian expedition of the Academy of Sciences of the U.S.S.R., which worked in the area due to be flooded after the completion of the Aswan Dam. Near the village of Dakka and in the Wadi Allaqi Gorge, through which an ancient road led to the gold mines, the expedition's members studied inscriptions carved in the rocks giving indications to prospectors for precious stones and gold during the Old and Middle King-

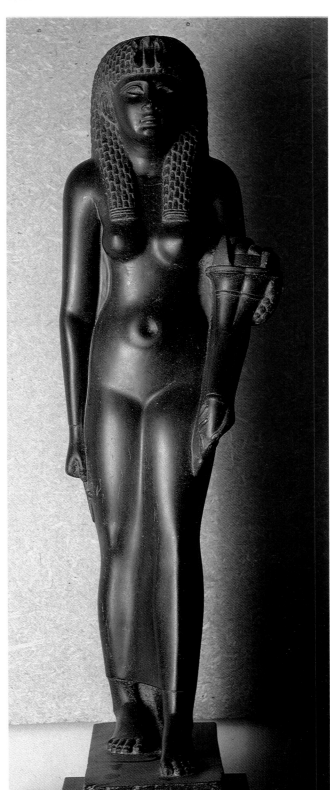

Papyrus:
The Tale of the Shipwrecked Man.
Total length 3.8 meters.
Nineteenth century B.C. Detail.

Statue of Arsinoë II.
Gabbro. Height 104.7 cm.
Third century B.C.
Acquired in 1929 from
the Peterhof palace of the
Duke of Leuchtenberg.

The archaic period of Persian civilization, which was more or less contemporary with the rise of the Egyptian state, spanning the late fourth and early third millennia B.C., is represented by a small but carefully selected collection of ceramics from the excavations at Susa, the capital of Elam, carried out by Jacques de Morgan and Toscano toward the end of the

1. Cylinder seal and its impression, showing a human-headed bull fighting a lion and a hero making a libation. Black steatite. Length 3.2 cm. Akkad, twenty-second century B.C. The name of the scribe Kaku also appears.

2. Soldiers: fragment of a relief from the palace of the Assyrian king Tiglath-pileser III (745–727 B.C.) in Kalhu (modern Nimrud), Iraq. Limestone. 82 × 77 cm.

1

2

nineteenth century. (Jacques de Morgan, who became a famous archaeologist and made important discoveries regarding the ancient history of the Orient, began his career in Russia as an engineer in the copper-smelting plant at Alaverdi in Transcaucasia.) The Susa ceramics collection consists of tall beakers and bowls with geometric designs and stylized animal figures: goats with enormous horns, rows of birds, and dogs.

The museum also possesses a large collection of Mesopotamian cuneiform texts dating from the Sumerian to the late Babylonian civilization. The oldest stone tablet, with hieroglyphic writing that predates cuneiform, belongs to the end of the fourth millennium B.C. Of particular interest are the small clay tablets from the Nikolai Likhachev collection, which formed part of the accounts kept in the famous Sumerian archives of the city of Lagash (the period of Urukagina and his successors, late twenty-fourth and early twenty-third centuries B.C.), and in those of the rival city of Umma (twenty-first century B.C.). These tablets bear witness not only to the economic life of the ancient Sumerians but also to their culture in general. Of great interest also is a fragment of a Hittite clay tablet engraved with the text of a treaty made between a Hittite king and the pharaoh Ramses II (thirteenth century B.C.).

The pieces from the ancient Middle East also include a good collection of seals from Mesopotamia, Asia Minor, and Central Asia, ranging from the irregularly shaped Sumerian seals to Persian examples of the Achaemenian period. Most of these have been

3. Cauldron ornament
in the form of a siren.
Bronze. 24 × 9 cm.
Urartu, eighth century B.C.
Found by Kurds in a tomb opposite
the Russian border post of Alishar
on the Araks River. Acquired
in 1859.

4. Priest with a pomegranate
branch: fragment of a relief from
the palace of the Assyrian king
Sargon II (722–705 B.C.) in Dur
Sharrukin (modern Khorsabad), Iraq.
Limestone. 106 × 46 cm.

5. Cauldron ornament
in the form of a bull's head.
Bronze. 11 × 5.5 cm.
Urartu, eighth century B.C.
Found by Kurds in a tomb opposite
the Russian border post of Alishar
on the Araks River. Acquired
in 1859.

bought from other collections, but some have come directly from excavations in the Caucasus and Central Asia and from Scythian barrows. Especially fine is the collection of Sumerian, Old Babylonian, Khurrite, and Assyrian glyptics. These remarkable examples of ancient art, and especially the cylindrical seals with their intricate engravings, provide valuable information about the mythology of the ancient Middle East.

In the 1860s the Hermitage acquired some stone reliefs from the Assyrian palaces of Ashurnasirpal II (ninth century B.C.) and of Tiglath-pileser III and Sargon II (both eighth century B.C.), which for a long time were displayed in the Ancient Egyptian rooms.

Especially impressive are the reliefs from the palace of Ashurnasirpal, depicting the king in the company of a god.

A contemporary and rival of Assyrian culture was the ancient state of Urartu (thirteenth to seventh centuries B.C.), the center of which was near Lake Van in modern Turkey. In 1859 the first examples of the art of this culture were brought to the Hermitage from a plundered tomb in northwestern Iran near the Russian border post of Alishar. They consisted of decorative elements from bronze cauldrons in the form of a bull's head and a winged female figure. At that time nothing was known about the ancient state of Urartu;

these objects were correctly identified only ninety-nine years later with the discovery, during the restoration of a bronze bell, of an inscription of the Urartian king Argishti I.

In the 1880s the Hermitage acquired some wonderful bronze figurines of imaginary creatures. Discovered near Lake Van, these pieces had originally been gold-plated and used to decorate a throne. One of the most interesting items is a winged lion with a human body and a face of white stone. When the throne was discovered, its separate parts were distributed among a number of museums: the Hermitage, the British Museum, the Louvre, the Berlin Museum, and the Metropolitan Museum in New York.

The greater part of the Hermitage collection comes from excavations at the site of the ancient citadel of Teishebaini (Karmir Blur, Erevan), which the museum carried out between 1939 and 1972 in collaboration with the Soviet Armenian Academy of Sciences. Razed by the Scythians in the early sixth century B.C., this citadel had underground wine cellars and storerooms containing wine, grain, and other objects and commodities, all of which have provided a clear idea of the economy of Urartu, as well as of its arts and crafts. Particularly noteworthy are a bronze shield with the figures of lions and bulls, a quiver showing chariots and horsemen, and some bronze drinking cups bearing the names of the Urartian kings of the eighth century B.C. These bowls of shining bronze are in a good state of preservation; each of them, when struck, rings out with its own clear note.

Also to be mentioned are the relics from Palmyra (Tadmor), an important staging post on the Roman trade routes through Syria. The Hermitage has a number of relief portraits obtained from tombs there, but its most valuable possession is a large stone slab, acquired in 1902, bearing the text of a 137 A.D. law written in both Greek and Aramaic. This law concerned trade in general, the method of levying duty on imports, and the taxes imposed on the various arts and crafts.

The department also exhibits a fine collection of Byzantine art from the fourth to the fifteenth centuries A.D. One special attraction is the collection of silver bowls and other vessels dating from the fifth to the seventh centuries, including outstanding examples of Byzantine carved and embossed work featuring scenes from ancient mythology, Christian motifs such as a cross flanked by two angels, and scenes of everyday life, as for instance a shepherd with his flock. Most of these were found at various times in the foothills of the Urals and in Siberia, and serve as proof of the thriving trade between the South with its art, and the North with its wealth of furs. On the back of a mid-sixth-century dish depicting Venus disguised as a shepherdess arriving at the tent of Anchises, there is a Sogdian inscription of the sixth or early seventh century that reads, "Dozoi, Lord of Bukhara," which shows how far north such objects could travel. Two other dishes depicting a snake and a horse have human figures, masks, and fish incised on them by their former owners. Of equal interest are the objects made of ivory (diptychs and pyxides), with delicately carved scenes from ancient myths and tragedies and the Bible.

Among the works of sculpture is the *Good Shepherd* (fourth to fifth centuries) and a large relief depicting circus scenes (sixth century) brought to Russia by Admiral G. A. Spiridov in 1774.

Gem with the inscription,
"Denak, Queen of Queens."
Amethyst. 2.3 × 1 cm.
Persia, third century A.D.
Denak was a daughter of
the Persian ruler Papak, and the
sister and first wife of Ardashir I,
founder of the Sassanid Dynasty.
Purchased in Georgia in the early
nineteenth century. Acquired from
the Stroganov collection, 1925.

Diptych with circus scenes.
Ivory. Height 33 cm,
width of each panel 10.5 cm.
Byzantium, fifth century A.D.
Acquired from the Bazilevsky
collection, 1885.

Pitcher with mythical figure
half dog, half bird.
Gilded silver. Height 33 cm.
Persia, sixth century A.D.
Found in a treasure near
the village of Pavlovka, Kharkov
Guberniya, Ukraine, in 1823.
Acquired from the Grand Duke Alexis
collection in Petersburg, 1912.

Dish depicting Ardashir III hunting.
Silver. Diam. 20.3 cm.
Persia, sixth century A.D.
Found in a treasure in the city of
Ufa, Bashkir Autonomous Republic,
1941.

Dish showing Prince Bahram Gor
and Azadeh hunting.
Gilded silver. Diam. 21.7 cm.
Persia, seventh century A.D.
Found in a treasure in the village
of Turushev, Kirov Oblast, 1927.

The second period of Byzantine art (tenth to fifteenth centuries A.D.) is also abundantly represented by ivory articles, ceramics, objects of applied art, and a great number of icons made of ivory, stone, and various metals, including some precious ones, decorated in enamel with the techniques known as *champlevé* and *cloisonné*.

Byzantine iconography is represented mostly by examples from the tenth to fifteenth centuries, often of exquisite workmanship. Especially famous is the 106-centimeter-high icon of Christ Pantocrator. At the lower corners are figures, unfortunately only partially preserved, of Alexis and John, who in 1363 founded the Temple of Christ on Mount Athos.

A large number of Byzantine objects have come to light during excavations north of the Black Sea, particularly in the Crimea. The earliest silver bowl, depicting the triumph of Constantine II, was found at Kerch in 1891, while the excavations at Chersonesus, in which the Hermitage always takes part, have produced a set of eleventh-century glazed ceramic bowls with rather primitive representations of birds, imaginary animals, and a man fighting a wild beast. Byzantine objects are constantly being found during excavations at Slavic and old Russian settlements, fortresses, and towns.

The Hermitage's large collection of relics from Coptic Egypt includes a world-famous selection of

fourth-to-sixth-century Coptic fabrics, with over three thousand examples of decorated cloth unique in style and design. Most of the items in the Coptic section have come at various times from a number of private collections, but some came directly from excavations carried out in Egypt by a Hermitage staff member, Vladimir Bock, who studied Coptic monasteries and necropolises there in 1888–89 and again in 1897–98.

Persian art is thoroughly represented in the museum. There were already some marvelous examples of the art of the Achaemenid Dynasty (sixth to fourth centuries B.C.) in Peter the Great's Kunstkammer. Other items in the same style were found during the

excavation of Scythian barrows, including a gold dagger handle representing a hunting scene from the Chertomlyk barrow, and a silver rhyton (a ritual drinking horn) with a tip in the shape of a winged goat, discovered in a barrow of the Seven Brothers group. A set of beautiful chalcedony seals includes a cylindrical one depicting the victory of an Achaemenid king over a pharaoh of Egypt. Other seals, belonging to the so-called Greco-Persian style of a later period, represent battle or hunting scenes.

The Hermitage takes special pride in its collection of Persian gold and silver wares of the Sassanid Dynasty (third to seventh centuries A.D.), especially remarkable because nearly all the pieces were found on Soviet territory—in the Urals and along the Kama River where they had originally been brought by traders—from the nineteenth century to the present day. Some Sassanian dishes were found on the sites of shaman sanctuaries, as witnessed by the drawings scratched on them, which resemble those mentioned in our description of Byzantine silver.

The story of these remarkable finds is full of amusing episodes, because those who first discovered these treasures more often than not failed to realize their value and simply took them home for their own use. Thus the treasure found in the region of Perm in 1872, which included a dish showing King Shapur II hunting boar, fell into the hands of a wealthy peasant. At first he refused to sell the things, declaring, "I use one dish for vodka and another for salt. The big one [the one depicting Shapur II] I'd like to use for cabbage soup, but the head and feet stick out and get in the way."

The collection of Sassanian dishes consists of fifty items that are really Sassanian and another sixty made in similar style. Especially fine are the dishes showing scenes of the kings hunting, or on their thrones in the midst of their retinues, or scenes illustrating episodes from epic poems, such as the hunt of Bahram Gor and Azadeh from Firdusi's epic, *Shah Namah*. Other dishes are decorated with pictures of animals, often imaginary ones such as the *senmur* (half dog, half bird). Recently the antiquarian market has been flooded with fake Sassanian articles; the Hermitage exhibits, whose authenticity is beyond dispute, provide an invaluable criterion.

The museum's Sassanian collection also includes over nine hundred glyptics, among them an amethyst engraved with the portrait of Queen Denak (third century) and a carnelian seal belonging to a priest named Khosrav (fourth century), both of them masterpieces of this specialized art. The collection of Sassanian coins, obtained largely from excavations, is of considerable scholarly interest.

Persian art of the twelfth to fifteenth centuries is represented by a good selection of metalwork and ceramics. One of the most important art centers was the

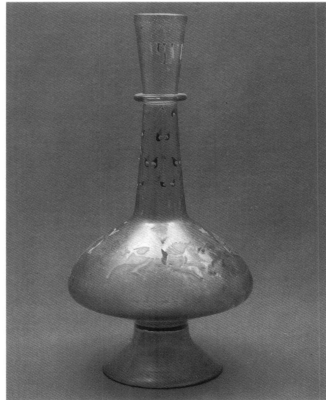

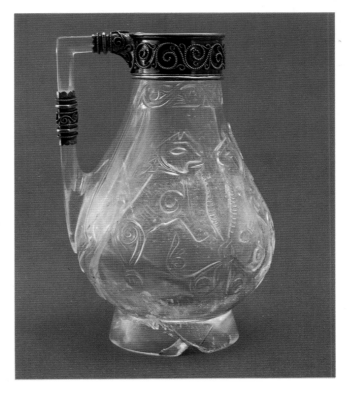

Censer in the form of
a snow leopard.
Bronze with copper and silver
inlays. Height 45 cm, length 41.5 cm.
Persia, eleventh century.
Acquired in 1930.

Water jug in the form of
a zebu and her calf.
Bronze inlaid with silver.
Height 31 cm.
Persia, 1206.
Acquired from an antique dealer,
1929; formerly in the Khanenko
collection in Kiev.

Pot.
Bronze with red copper and silver
inlays. Height 18 cm.
Herat, 1163. Made by Muhammad
ibn Abd al-Vahid and by Masud ibn
Ahmad an-Nakkash.
Acquired from the Bobrinsky
collection in Leningrad, 1926.

Lamp.
Rock crystal. Length 22 cm.
Egypt, tenth century.

Pitcher.
Enameled and gilt glass.
Height 33 cm.
Syria (Damascus?),
fourteenth century. Found during
N. I. Veselovsky's excavations
in the village of Belorechenskaya,
northern Caucasus.

Pitcher.
Rock crystal. Height 19.8 cm.
Egypt, tenth to eleventh centuries
(metal parts from a later period).
Acquired from the S.G. Stroganov
collection in Rome, 1911.

city of Herat (now in Afghanistan), which produced, among other objects in the collection, a bronze pot with scenes of feudal life and inscriptions, all executed in red copper with silver inlays. An inscription gives us the date of manufacture (1163 by the Western calendar) and the names of the owner, the original client, and the two craftsmen who made it.

During the twelfth and thirteenth centuries the cities of Kashan and Rey became famous for their production of ceramics. Especially beautiful are the multicolored bowls and goblets (*minai*), with human figures set in highly ornamental frames, along with short poetic inscriptions and wishes for good luck. Of great

interest are the highly polished tiles from the thirteenth-century Imamzada Yahya mausoleum in the town of Varamin in central Iran, featuring not only pictorial designs but texts from both the Koran and Firdusi's *Shah Namah*. Other tiles of the same type have quotations from Nizami's epic poem *Laila and Majnun*. A most splendid example of Kashan craftsmanship is the thirteenth-century luster vase showing polo players on horseback, musicians, and animals lurking in a thicket.

Among the many bronze items in this section are the censers and water jugs. One, an eagle-shaped censer, bears an inscription in Kufic Arabic giving the

name of the craftsman and the date (796), while another censer, also with an Arabic inscription but dating from the twelfth century, is in the shape of a snow leopard. A third item, a jug in the form of a zebu with her calf, has a lion-shaped handle and a Persian inscription dating it 1206. All three pieces are beautifully worked, and it is singularly appropriate that the inscription on the jug tells us that the three figures "were cast at one time."

Persian art of the fifteenth to eighteenth centuries is represented by carpets, silk fabrics, miniatures, ceramics, and glass. The collection of medieval articles from Syria and Egypt, on the other hand, is far smaller than the Persian collection, but contains objects of great value obtained from private collections. A magnificent large vessel made of cut rock crystal and showing a pair of lions facing each other dates from the tenth to eleventh centuries, the time of the Egyptian Fatimids. The neck and handle have gold inlays and reliefs representing ears of grain. It is hard to imagine the pains the craftsman must have taken to do such fine work in a material as hard as rock crystal.

In the description of Western European art below (p. 174), mention is made of a fourteenth-century Syrian glass horn, formerly on display in Peter the Great's Kunstkammer. Decorated with enameling showing Christian saints and two lines of writing in Arabic, this horn was brought to Europe by Crusaders and set in a fine silver mount in Augsburg in 1551.

Belonging to the later period of the Egyptian Mamelukes is a splendid glass lamp, decorated with multicolored enamels and with an inscription bearing the name of the sultan Muzaffar Hadji, who ruled for a mere fifteen months in 1346–47. Thus, rare for the work of Syrian glass blowers of that time, it can be dated with absolute precision. Moreover, the lamp is especially interesting because fragments of similar Syrian glassware were found during excavations at Sarai-Berke, the capital of the Golden Horde on the Volga.

The rulers of the Mameluke Dynasty originally came from the steppes of southern Russia and the Caucasus. In their efforts to resist the Mongol thrust through Central Asia into the Middle East, they es-

tablished close links with the Golden Horde, the rivals of the Great Horde. As early as 1262 the founder of the Mameluke Dynasty, Baybars I, sent the first Egyptian mission to Sarai-Berke by way of Constantinople and the Crimea, thus initiating relations between Egypt and the Golden Horde that lasted until the end of the fourteenth century. Excavations at Sarai-Berke and, particularly, at tombs near the village of Belorechenskaya in the Krasnodar area, as well as in the Caucasus, have yielded many fragments and whole glass vessels decorated with colored enamels and gold—concrete archaeological evidence of what had already been inferred from written sources.

Horn-shaped vessel with Christian saints and a Kufic inscription. Colored enamels on glass. Height 29.5 cm. Syria, fourteenth century. The silver mounts were commissioned in Augsburg by Bruno von Drollschagen in 1551. From Peter the Great's Kunstkammer.

Goblet. Faïence painted with colored enamels. Height 11.5 cm. Minai pottery of Persia. Transferred from the Stieglitz Museum, 1925.

Lamp with enameling on glass. Egypt, fourteenth century. It bears the heraldic emblem of Sultan al-Melik al-Muzaffar Hadji. Acquired in 1885.

Three rooms in the Oriental Department are devoted to the culture and art of Turkey from the fifteenth to the early nineteenth centuries. The exhibits include sixteenth-century ceramics and tiles from the town of Iznik, with their characteristic combination of white, red, and dark and light blues, as well as carpets, fabrics, metalwork, and weapons. Of special interest are the Turkish fabrics of the sixteenth and seventeenth centuries, when the Ottoman Empire established trade relations with Italy and so began to feel the influence of Europe. Also evident are signs of the long-established trade with Russia, which brought the latter the expensive brocaded fabrics that were used, among other things, for clerical vestments. A fine example is the seventeenth-century chasuble of Turkish brocade with Russian-made shoulder pieces, formerly owned by the boyar Trubetskoy.

Exhibits devoted to Far Eastern culture are found on the third floor of the Winter Palace. This display acquaints us with the different peoples and tribes who, living far from Western Europe, always strove to maintain contact with the rest of the Far East, as well as with the Middle East and Europe, even as early as the Scythian period. Evidence of caravan routes, including the so-called Silk Route, can be found from the second century B.C. right down to the sixteenth century A.D., when the routes were superseded by the

Riza-i-Abbasi.
Miniature.
Indian ink and gold on paper.
14.8 × 8.4 cm.
Persia, 1602–03.
Transferred from the Stieglitz
Museum, 1924.

newly discovered trade routes through the southern seas. The tribes that lived along these land routes exploited their situation by exchanging cattle for the goods transported by the caravans.

The most valuable merchandise so transported was indeed Chinese silk, but this was by no means the only article of exchange in a trade long dominated by Persian and Sogdian merchants. The provinces of Sinkiang and Kansu in northwestern China, as well as Inner Mongolia, were important centers along this route. In the second half of the nineteenth century Russian travelers and scientists obtained a mass of in-

formation and managed to preserve a number of cultural monuments made of loess, the fragile, fine yellowish-brown earth widely used for building in northern China.

In 1924–25, at Noin-Ula in Mongolia, the Russian traveler Pëtr Kozlov discovered a number of barrows belonging to Hunnish chiefs of the first centuries B.C. and A.D. The burial chambers were of unusual magnificence, their wooden walls and floors entirely lined with woolen carpets decorated with an appliqué representing a winged dragon attacking a deer. This motif resembles those found in the more ancient barrows at Pazyryk in the Altai Mountains. The coffins were sheathed in silk adorned with gold sequins. Silver plaques showing a yak standing between two pines on a mountaintop are reminiscent of an old Uighur legend about one of the forefathers of their tribe, who was said to be a yak-king. The Noin-Ula tombs yielded Chinese, Iranian, and indigenous objects, the last noticeably inferior to the others.

The date of these tumuli was established on the basis of a Chinese inscription on a lacquered bowl, which gave the year of its manufacture, 2 A.D., as well as the names of the craftsmen. The fabrics, including the clothing of the dead, were well preserved, thanks to the flooding of these barrows by underground water. At Khotan in Sinkiang Province, a focal point of trade between the Far East and India and Central Asia, Nikolai Petrovsky found a number of second- and third-century A.D. terra-cotta statues and vessels decorated with painted figures and moldings.

Belonging to a later period are the murals and clay sculptures from the oases of Kucha and Turfan. A statue from Kucha (sixth to seventh centuries A.D.) represents a merchant in a luxurious gown, perhaps of ermine, while the small statues of infantrymen and cavalry from Turfan recall the veritable army of life-size clay figures of warriors and horses discovered in 1974 near the mausoleum of the Chinese emperor Qin-shi-huang-di, who ruled in the second half of the third century B.C. Extremely impressive too are the monumental ninth-century frescoes discovered at Turfan, in the land of the Uighurs, and some wonderful fragments of murals of the same period from Shikshim in the Karashahr Oasis.

A great deal of material was brought to light in Kansu Province during excavations carried out in 1909–10 and 1914–15, under the direction of Sergei Oldenburg, at the monastery of Qian-fo-dong ("the Cave of a Thousand Buddhas"). Situated near Dunhuang, and built in the fourth century on the old Silk Route, this monastery was in use until the eleventh century, and during that long period housed a vast number of sculptures, paintings, and written texts. Particularly striking are two large eighth-century loess figures of imaginary animals, "guardians of the throne of Buddha." More like lions than anything else, with their fangs bared, one painted black and the other red, they must surely have been an awe-inspiring sight. The sculpted figures of monks and deities from the same monastery belong to the ninth and tenth centuries. The clay sculptures and murals from Sinkiang and Kansu were brought to the Hermitage in 1934 in very poor condition, and the museum's specialists put a great deal of time and effort into their restoration.

In 1933 the Ethnographic Museum presented the Hermitage with invaluable materials from the expeditions of 1908 and 1926 led by Pëtr Kozlov, who directed the excavation of the ancient city of Khara Khoto (Ichin), built by the Chinese on the northern edge of the Gobi Desert as a defense against the nomads. In the eleventh century the town passed into the hands of the Tanguts, and then the Mongols, until the Chinese destroyed it during their war against the Mongols in 1372. The desert sands then buried the abandoned town right up to the top of its walls, so that Kozlov's expeditions found a wealth of well-preserved material — tools and implements, ceramics, porcelain, fabrics, and the world's earliest paper money, which dates from the fourteenth century.

Particularly interesting finds were made at the *suburgan* (mausoleum-temple) outside the city walls, which yielded vast numbers of clay statues of various sizes. Stored in the largest of them were many icons on canvas, silk, and paper, painted in the Chinese and Tibetan styles, as well as books printed from wood blocks. Worthy of mention is a fine portrait of a civil servant, drawn in India ink and colored with tempera, dating from the eleventh or twelfth century, the flowering of Chinese painting. As the 1908 expedition was a small one, without sufficient manpower to move the statues, these were photographed and buried again. By the time the 1926 expedition returned to the spot, the sands had shifted so much that it proved impossible to find them.

The Hermitage possesses many examples of Chinese art of the fifteenth to eighteenth centuries, including porcelain intended for export to Europe, and to Russia in particular. A large collection of Chinese lacquered paintings was donated to the Hermitage by the academician Vasili Alekseev, a leading expert on Chinese culture. The display is rounded off by works of some twentieth-century artists such as Qi Bai-shi and Xu Bei-hong.

The Hermitage also has a modest display of Indian, Indonesian, and Japanese art.

The earliest Caucasian exhibits in the Oriental Department are archaeological finds dating from the Bronze Age and the beginning of the Iron Age (eleventh to eighth centuries B.C.). This was a culture formed largely of livestock-breeding tribes that developed a high degree of civilization and had relations with the various countries of the ancient Orient. Throughout Transcaucasia bronze objects such as swords, daggers, axes, spearheads, and arrowheads tended to be very similar, for they came from common

metalworking centers located near the copper mines and were used for barter among the tribes, whereas household utensils and especially pottery exhibit great variety, having local characteristics. All objects of this kind in the Hermitage came to the museum in the late nineteenth century from the excavations of the Imperial Archaeological Commission. Today, now that the Transcaucasian republics have started their own archaeological research programs (their findings have established the dates of the ancient Caucasian cultures), the Hermitage collection has lost much of its former preeminence.

All the same, the museum does contain a few

Shah Jahan's protecting ring
for archery.
Gold inset with rubies, emeralds,
and diamonds (the largest 9 carats).
4.2 × 3.4 cm.
India, seventeenth century.
Presented to Empress Anna by
Nadir Shah in 1741, together with
other jewelry. In the Winter
Palace collection in the
eighteenth century.

Jug inset with emeralds.
Height 26.5 cm.
India, seventeenth century.
Presented to Empress Anna by
Nadir Shah in 1741, together with
other jewelry. In the Winter
Palace collection in the
eighteenth century.

unique items, especially those from Khodzhali and Archadzor in Azerbaijan. The 1895 excavations of the Khodzhali barrow in mountainous Karabakh yielded an agate bead with an Assyrian inscription mentioning the name of King Adadnirari I, who reigned at the beginning of the thirteenth century B.C., but the majority of the objects found in the tomb cannot be earlier than the eleventh century B.C. During the recent excavation of a tomb in Armenia of about the same date as the one at Khodzhali, an agate weight weighing one shekel was found. Shaped like a frog, it bears a cuneiform inscription of the Kassite Dynasty of Babylonia, including the name of King Ulamburiash I, who

reigned at the end of the sixteenth century B.C. The fact that these objects were found in tombs of much later date can be explained easily enough, for the livestock-raising tribesmen were in the habit of pillaging older tombs which, as we have learned from recent excavations, were exceedingly rich in gold and silver. The Transcaucasian culture of the second millennium B.C., however, is not represented in the Hermitage.

The advance of Bronze Age culture in Transcaucasia was halted in the eighth century B.C., when the southern parts of the area were overrun by the state of Urartu. The Hermitage has no antiquities from the post-Urartian or Hellenistic periods or from the time

Fragment of a wall painting from the Indian Hall of the Varakhsha palace near Bukhara. Sogdiana, eighth century. Excavations by V. A. Shishkin on the site of ancient Varakhsha, Uzbekistan, 1949–54.

when new states were forming in Armenia, Georgia, and Azerbaijan.

Certain individual objects meriting attention belong to the Roman period (first to second centuries A.D.). Among these are the Syrian goblet of ruby-colored glass with a rim of chased silver, found at Mtskheta in Georgia; earrings, rings, and the gold bracelets set with garnets from the village of Ashnak in Armenia; the capital of a pillar from a first-century temple at Garni in Armenia; and a second-century A.D. silver dish with the figure of a Nereid flanked by Triton and Eros, found in 1893 at the village of Enkigond in Azerbaijan.

There is a much richer collection from the early

Middle Ages (fourth to eighth centuries), the time of the Sassanid Dynasty in Persia, and from the later medieval period (ninth and tenth centuries). It consists of small icons, settings for icons, and glazed ceramics from Georgia; ceramics from the medieval Armenian towns of Dvin and Ani; twelfth- and thirteenth-century bronze mortars excavated from the fortress of Anberd on Mount Aragats; and a fourteenth-century relief from the church at Noravank (Yekhegnadzor) with portraits of Armenian feudal lords of the Proshyan family who built the church.

The *pièce de résistance* of the Armenian collection is a silver icon with three folding panels representing the

Fragment of a shield showing a horseman.
Wood covered with leather.
61 × 23 cm.
Sogdiana, early eighth century.
Found at Mug, Tadzhikistan, in 1933.
Excavations by the Academy of Sciences of the U.S.S.R. under A. A. Freiman.

Horsemen:
fragment of a wall painting from a house in ancient Pendzhikent.
160 × 150 cm.
Sogdiana, early eighth century.
Acquired in 1951. Excavations by Aleksandr Yakubovsky in Pendzhikent, Tadzhikistan.

Annunciation and various saints. The lower part of the right-hand panel shows the Armenian king Hethum II at prayer, while an inscription tells us that this icon was made in Cilicia in 1293. Medieval Armenian art is also represented by twelfth- and thirteenth-century illuminated manuscripts.

Of particular interest among the ceramics are the twelfth- and thirteenth-century vessels unearthed at the town of Orenkala (ancient Bailakan in Azerbaijan). Glazed in unusual brown and green colors, they are also quite distinctive in subject matter, showing a hunter shooting with a bow and arrow, or a mounted huntsman in regal attire. These vessels often bear the

name of the craftsman and the owner. The Oriental Department also has some twelfth-to-fourteenth-century stone reliefs from the village of Kubachi in the mountains of Dagestan. They show hunting scenes and duels between knights on horseback and often have imitations of Arabic inscriptions. The same site also produced some highly ornamented bronze cauldrons and fine glazed ceramics.

An overall view of the objects found in the northern Caucasus shows that this area formed a kind of bridge between the Middle East and Eastern Europe, being crossed by the trade routes that later formed the Silk Route and its branches. Superb painted glass vessels from Syria and Venice have been found over the years in the tombs of Ossetian tribes, while similar objects, including a Syrian glass bottle with figures of horsemen in colored enamel and an Italian pitcher with painted decorations such as fish scales, have been found in a fourteenth-century tomb in the village of Belorechenskaya on the Kuban River.

Also to be mentioned is the unique collection of seventh-to-ninth-century fabrics found in the North Caucasian burial grounds of the Alani and Adyg tribes, and particularly the Moshchevaya Balka tomb on the Bolshaya Laba River near the Kuban River. This tumulus also yielded a wonderful and exceptionally well-preserved caftan made of Sogdian silk; with its mythical creatures (half dog, half bird), the design is similar to the design on the robes of the Sassanid king Khosrau II of Persia as he appears in the famous Taq-i-Bustan relief. It was along the trade routes through the Caucasus that Byzantine, Sogdian, and Chinese silks found their way north. On rare occasions whole costumes were made of this silk, but more frequently only small pieces of it were used to decorate clothes made of local materials, as in the case of the Coptic decorative fabrics.

The trade routes through the Caucasus are mentioned by the sixth-century Byzantine historian Menander and also by Chinese sources. Confirmation of contact with China is provided by Chinese objects discovered in the Moshchevaya Balka tomb, including fragments of a painting on silk of a horseman and a scrap of paper showing accounts written in Chinese. These rather surprising discoveries bear witness to the extent of trade between East and West at an early date.

The culture of Central Asia is represented at the Hermitage by items from various periods and regions, starting from the third millennium B.C. Sites in southern Turkmenia have yielded evidence of an early agricultural society linked to areas still farther to the south. Prominent among these finds are ceramics bearing geometrical designs and occasionally the figures of animals. The museum's display of fabrics, ceramics, and human figures worked in clay comes from excavations carried out by the Academy of Sciences of

Jug with painted ducks. Terra cotta with painting under glaze. Height 29 cm. Central Asia, eleventh century. Transferred from the Stieglitz Museum.

the U.S.S.R. in the ruins of the city of Kara Tepe. Livestock-breeding cultures also existed in those times in central and northern Central Asia. The relations between the agricultural and livestock-raising cultures to a large extent conditioned the history of the region. Relations between the southern and the northern cultures can be traced with the help of the second-millennium B.C. treasure found in the Fergana Valley, which includes a bronze pin with a group sculpture on the upper part of it depicting the milking of a cow.

While Scythian culture was developing in Eastern Europe, the related Saka culture was gaining ground in Central Asia. It is represented by a number of objects found at burial sites, including a large rectangular sacrificial altar made of bronze from the Fertile Crescent, the altar's rim decorated with figures of imaginary animals.

The political history of Central Asia during the first millennium B.C. profoundly affected the development of art and culture in the area. During the sixth to fourth centuries B.C. a large part of Central Asia was included in the Persian Empire of the Achaemenids, but in the fourth century it was conquered by Alexander the Great, and after his death in 323 B.C. passed into the hands of the Seleucids. In the third century B.C. the two empires of Parthia and Bactria were established in Central Asia, but were eventually superseded by the Kushan Empire of the first to fourth centuries A.D. These phases in Central Asian history are reflected in this section of the museum, above all in the collection of coins, but also in various objects from a variety of places.

The celebrated frieze from the Temple of Airtam, donated to the Hermitage by the Uzbek Republic, belongs to the Kushan period, specifically to the first century A.D. It depicts groups of musicians in a setting of acanthus leaves. The relief work is executed in an unusual style, combining ancient tradition with elements derived from India, as is typical of Kushan art.

Architectural monuments ranging from the third century B.C. to the third century A.D. were discovered in the ancient Parthian city of Nisa, near Ashkhabad, where the excavations carried out by Mikhail Masson also yielded numerous objects exemplifying the culture of the time. The Hermitage possesses fragments of a clay frieze from one of the ceremonial halls, decorated with a battlementlike motif, and two rhytons of ivory, the rhytons' upper parts decorated with reliefs of scenes from ancient mythology, their lower parts carved in the form of imaginary winged creatures. Also displayed are clay shards (*ostraka*) with inscriptions in Aramaic characters, which form part of the large archive discovered at Nisa.

In the 1930s a permanent archaeological expedition under the direction of Sergei Tolstov was organized to study the ancient culture of Khorezm, a vast area south of the Aral Sea. This proved to be an event

Rhyton with base in the form of a fantastic animal.
Ivory. Parthia,
second to first centuries B.C.
Excavations by Mikhail Masson in Nisa, near Ashkhabad, 1948.
A gift from the Turkmen Republic.

of paramount importance in Central Asian archaeology. Objects dating from various periods have come to light, but the items in the Hermitage represent only one of these, the third to fourth centuries A.D., and a single source, the great palace of the kings of Khorezm, the ruins of which had long lain buried under the Toprak Kale temple in the Kyzyl Kym Desert. Excavations were carried on there in 1938 and 1940, and again in 1945–50. The rooms of the palace were found to be decorated with frescoes and painted clay sculptures. Especially magnificent was the hall adorned with almost life-size statues of the king and his courtiers and with figures of warriors half that size. Unfortunately, these statues were made of fragile materials and have come down to us badly broken; even so, the pieces — especially the heads of the warriors in a fair state of preservation — give us a good idea of the art of Khorezm in the third century A.D.

The Hermitage has considerable material from digs at the Sogdian town of Pendzhikent in Tadzhikistan, which flourished from the sixth to eighth centuries. Work began here in 1947 and is still going on, with expeditions organized by the Academy of Sciences of the U.S.S.R., the Tadzhik Academy of Sciences, and experts from the Hermitage led by Aleksandr Yakubovsky, Mikhail Dyakonov, and Aleksandr Belenitsky. These excavations have revealed the various layers of the town, disclosing its streets and individual buildings, which include not only temples but the houses of well-to-do citizens.

Pendzhikent is particularly well known for its colorful frescoes, which have required a great deal of restoration. Hermitage restoration teams have been using previously untried methods to detach the frescoes from the damp walls of buildings, free them from damaging salts, and preserve or partially restore the colors. While work continues, only a small sample of this early medieval art is on display.

These frescoes express not only religious (that is, Buddhist) but also secular themes, such as scenes from epic poems or even fairy tales. The same character often appears in different scenes and situations inspired by a narrative that is as yet unknown to us. In one hall of the Hermitage is a fresco that occupied an entire wall twelve meters long: it represents the victory of a legendary hero over a dragon and a battle between warriors and evil spirits.

One cycle of frescoes is based on tales resembling Aesop's fables. For example, there is the story of the fool who killed the goose that laid golden eggs, and another of a hare who persuaded a lion to leap at its own reflection on a wall. These are all exceptionally fine examples of Sogdian art of the seventh and eighth centuries.

Ceremonial rooms in Pendzhikent were also decorated with wooden panels showing horsemen framed in foliage, and with columns in the form of dancing

Funerary statuette of a merchant.
Terra cotta and wood.
Kucha Oasis, Sinkiang, sixth to seventh centuries.
From Sergei Oldenburg's first Turkestan expedition, 1909–10.

girls. Since the wooden artifacts found in the city had been carbonized, much restoration work was needed to make them fit for display. There are also fragments of a clay frieze from the courtyard of a temple, showing fish and sea monsters among the waves. This work was probably connected with the cult of the Zeravshan River, which was of prime importance to the town. Founded in the sixth century, Pendzhikent at the beginning of the eighth century became the capital of a small principality ruled by Prince Divastich, leader of a revolt against the Arabs who had conquered the area. In 721–22 the prince was defeated in battle and withdrew with a small force to a castle on a rock at Mug, in an almost inaccessible area on the upper reaches of the Zeravshan. But the odds were against him; eventually he was forced to surrender.

Excavations at this castle in 1933 brought to light some interesting archaeological material that found its way to the Hermitage, including household utensils in wood, leather, and metal, pieces of Sogdian and Chinese silk, and arrow shafts. Outstanding among these objects is the central part of a leather-covered wooden shield, with a well-preserved painting of a horseman in the style of the Pendzhikent frescoes. Also displayed in this section of the museum are certain documents from the archives that Divastich kept in his last mountain refuge. Most of them are written in the Sogdian language on leather, wood, or Chinese paper.

The Hermitage also possesses a fresco from the palace of the king of Bukhara (seventh to eighth centuries), discovered during the 1938 and 1954 excavations of the ancient town of Varakhsha. This ornamental fresco repeats the motif of the king seated on an elephant and fighting snow leopards, tigers, and imaginary winged dragons. In the Pendzhikent frescoes a dark-blue background predominates, whereas at Varakhsha the heraldic figures are painted on a background of red.

The culture of the peoples of Central Asia during the ninth to twelfth centuries is richly represented by glazed ceramics and glass and metal wares. In the 1220s Central Asia was conquered by Genghis Khan and his Mongol hordes; a great number of his followers formed a new state, the Golden Horde, with its capital at Sarai-Berke on the Volga. The Oriental Department contains materials found during the excavation of this ancient city.

Some exhibits date from the second half of the fourteenth century when Timur, known in the West as Tamerlane or Tamburlaine, unified the whole of Central Asia under his rule. This period witnessed a great deal of large-scale building, especially in Samarkand, the capital of the region, to which artists and craftsmen were brought by force from other areas. The Hermitage has a stone tablet bearing an inscription in both Arabic and Mongol; it commemorates

Tamerlane's campaign in 1391 against Tokhtamysh, Khan of the Golden Horde. Also of special interest is an enormous bronze water vessel (about 2.5 meters in diameter) made on Tamerlane's orders in 1399 by Persian craftsmen and intended for the Ahmad Yasavi mosque in Turkestan, in the present-day Soviet republic of Kazakhstan. The inscription on it gives us the date of manufacture as well as the name of its maker: Abd-al-Aziz of Tabriz.

Tamerlane was buried at Samarkand in the majestic Gur-i-Mir mausoleum, which was begun during his reign and completed in the fifteenth century. The Hermitage possesses a carved wooden door from this mausoleum, well known from the painting by Vasili Vereshchagin, and a mosaic inscription from above one of the entrances to the mausoleum itself. The door is exquisitely carved and inlaid with mother-of-pearl, ebony, rosewood, ivory, silver, and red copper. The Arabic inscriptions comment on the transitory nature of earthly joys. The brief mosaic inscription reads: "This is the tomb of the Sultan of the World, the emir Timur, son-in-law of the emir Hussein." This emphasizes Tamerlane's connection with the family of Genghis Khan, of which Hussein was a descendant.

This description of the section dealing with the culture of Central Asia has mentioned only the most

Funerary statuette of a horseman.
Terra cotta and wood. Height 36 cm.
Turfan Oasis, Sinkiang, tenth to eleventh centuries.
From Sergei Oldenburg's first Turkestan expedition, 1909–10.

Funerary statuette of a servant.
Terra cotta and wood.
Height 28.5 cm.
Turfan Oasis, Sinkiang, tenth to
eleventh centuries.

Funerary statuette of a warrior.
Terra cotta and wood.
Height 24 cm.
Turfan Oasis, Sinkiang, tenth to
eleventh centuries.

Female funerary statuette.
Terra cotta and wood.
Height 26 cm.
Turfan Oasis, Sinkiang, tenth to
eleventh centuries.

outstanding works and has left out items representing the Central Asian peoples of the fifteenth to nineteenth centuries, which nevertheless include some fine examples of illuminated manuscripts (Firdusi's *Shah Namah* and Nizami's *Khamsa,* copied for the Persian ruler Shahrukh in 1431), as well as ceramics, finely worked metal vessels, weapons, and rugs of the eighteenth and nineteenth centuries.

Finally I should mention the Oriental Department's Special Storeroom, created in 1960 for articles of particular value. Preserved here is the jewelry presented in 1741 to Empress Anna by Nadir Shah, the Persian conqueror of India. It includes a large gold

ring worn to protect the thumb while drawing a bow, which once belonged to Shah Jahan (1628–58) of the Mogul Dynasty, builder of the Taj Mahal. The ring is decorated with rubies and emeralds and is set with five diamonds, the largest of which weighs nine carats. Also in the Special Storeroom is a Persian saber bearing the name of Fath Ali Shah that once belonged to Alexander II. The hilt and scabbard are studded with 2,500 diamonds and over 700 emeralds. A particularly splendid aigrette made to crown a Turkish turban, adorned with diamonds, pearls, and ostrich feathers, is said to have been presented to Admiral Fëdor Ushakov.

Monks and bodhisattvas:
fragment of a mural.
105 × 98 cm.
Shikshim monastery in
the Karashahr Oasis, Sinkiang,
ninth to tenth centuries.
All the above from Sergei Oldenburg's
first Turkestan expedition, 1909–10.

Fragment of mural. 65 × 87 cm.
Shikshim monastery in the Karashahr Oasis, Sinkiang,
ninth to tenth centuries.
From Sergei Oldenburg's first Turkestan expedition, 1909–10.

Head of Buddha.
Terra cotta. Height 23 cm.
Site of ancient
Idikut-Shari, near Turfan, eighth to ninth centuries.
From the Turkestan collection of Sergei Oldenburg.

Two-headed Buddha.
Terra cotta. Height 58 cm.
Khara Khoto, twelfth century.
Excavations by Pëtr Kozlov, 1907.

The Department of Western European Art

The picture gallery is the oldest and most popular department in the museum, and it is only natural that the purchase of the first collection of pictures for the Winter Palace is regarded as marking the foundation of the Hermitage as a whole. In 1764 the Winter Palace took delivery of 225 works that had been bought a year earlier in Germany from the art dealer Gotzkowski for 180,000 Dutch guldens. Originally intended for sale to Frederick the Great, this collection consisted for the most part of Flemish and Dutch paintings, including such famous works as Frans Hals's *Portrait of a Young Man with a Glove* and Jan Steen's *Revelers.*

ITALIAN
13th and 14th centuries

Ugolino di Tedice.
Crucifix, c. 1270.
Tempera on wood. 90 × 62 cm. (The lower part of the cross is broken.)
Transferred from the Stroganov palace-museum in Leningrad, 1926.

Unknown master of the Venetian school.
Madonna of the *Annunciation,* late thirteenth to early fourteenth centuries.
Tempera on panel. 105 × 61.5 cm.
From the N. P. Likhachev collection; transferred from the Russian State Museum, 1923.

Even before that time the palaces of the czars had contained a wealth of paintings, including some by celebrated artists. During the building of the Winter Palace, Czarina Elizabeth had entertained the idea of gathering all the paintings from the palaces on the outskirts of Petersburg and assembling them in one place. But as these had been purchased rather haphazardly, they could never have formed an organic collection.

The acquisition of the Gotzkowski collection led to a spate of buying. Catherine the Great's correspondence with the French encyclopedists Diderot and Grimm, whom she consulted about extending her collection, sheds light on the beginnings of the Hermitage. Instructed by the empress to search for available works of art abroad, Russian diplomats became major participants at all international auctions.

The Russian court was represented in France by a young ambassador, Dmitri Golitsyn, a man of wide culture who later became an honorary member of the Petersburg Academy of Sciences. His personal contacts and friendships with leading public figures and artists in Paris contributed largely to the success of his mission. Such masterpieces as Rembrandt's *Return of*

the Prodigal Son and Poussin's *Tancred and Erminia* were acquired through his good offices in 1766. In the next two years two private collections were bought in Paris — those of Jean de Julienne and Louis-Jean Gaignat, the first of which consisted chiefly of paintings of the Dutch school. In 1768, again thanks to Golitsyn, the Winter Palace gallery acquired the collection of forty-six paintings, as well as a number of drawings, assembled by the Austrian minister Count Cobentzl at The Hague.

In Dresden in 1769 Prince Aleksandr Beloselsky bought a large collection from Count Heinrich von Brühl, a Saxon minister, who while assembling paint-

Unknown master of the Venetian school. *St. Giuliana of Collalto,* fourteenth century. St. Giuliana, founder and first abbess of the Santi Biagio e Cataldo Monastery of Giudecca, Venice, was canonized after 1297. Tempera on panel. 73 × 64.5 cm. Late Gothic frame. Four panels (28 × 30 cm each) from a polyptych. Transferred from the Russian State Museum, 1923.

109

Ugolino Lorenzetti.
Crucifixion.
Subject from Matthew 27: 31–56;
Mark 15: 20–41; Luke 23: 24–49;
John 19: 16–37.
Tempera on panel. 91.5 × 55.5 cm.
Acquired through the State Museum
Depository from Prince G. G. Gagarin's
collection in Petrograd, 1919.

Simone Martini.
Madonna of the *Annunciation*
(one panel of a diptych).
Tempera on panel. 30.5 × 21.5 cm.
From the S. G. Stroganov collection
in Rome, bequeathed in 1911.

111

ings for the Dresden picture gallery had not neglected to buy works of art on his own account, giving preference to the Dutch and Flemish schools. Among this group were *View of a Haarlem Suburb* by Philips Wouwerman and *Breakfast with Oysters* by Frans van Mieris.

The Winter Palace picture gallery spread to the newly built Little Hermitage as well as to the pavilion at the north end of the Hanging Garden, opened in February 1769. But even before the latter was finished, work had begun on the two galleries on either side of the garden, which were not completed until 1775.

The safe delivery of paintings to Petersburg was not always an easy matter: in 1771 the Brankamp col-

lection, bought in Amsterdam, went down with the ship that was carrying it. But this loss was made up for the following year in Paris, when Diderot and the Swiss political figure Jean-Robert Tronchin helped to ensure the purchase of the celebrated collection of Pierre Crozat (the Thiers Gallery), which had had an eventful history. Made up of works of various schools, it had been chosen with great taste and ability. Among its outstanding works were Giorgione's *Judith,* a *Holy Family* by Raphael, Rembrandt's *Danaë,* Veronese's *Adoration of the Magi* and *Pietà,* Van Dyck's *Portrait of a Man,* Sébastien Bourdon's *Death of Dido,* and Watteau's *Actors of the Comédie Française.* Eleven

ITALIAN
15th and 16th centuries

Fra Angelico (called Fra Beato).
*Madonna and Child with St. Dominic
and St. Thomas Aquinas,* 1424–30.
Fresco from San Domenico monastery
in Fiesole, near Florence.
196 × 187 cm.
Purchased in Florence from
the artists A. Mazzanti
and C. Conti in 1882.

Bartolomeo Caporali.
*Saints Francis of Assisi,
Herculaneus, Luke, and James
the Greater* (predella).
Tempera and oil on panel. 23 × 62 cm.
From the S. G. Stroganov
collection in Rome and the
Elia Volpi collection in Florence,
before 1910; transferred from the
Stroganov palace-museum in
Leningrad, 1926.

Bartolomeo Caporali.
*Saints Nicholas, Lawrence, Peter Martyr,
and Anthony of Padua* (predella).
Tempera and oil on panel. 23 × 62 cm.
From the S. G. Stroganov
collection in Rome and the
Elia Volpi collection in Florence,
before 1910; transferred from the
Stroganov palace-museum in
Leningrad, 1926.

paintings of this collection that had passed as the dowry of Crozat's daughter to Duke Etienne François de Choiseul were also bought at the time, including Murillo's *Boy with a Dog.* Certain other paintings arrived at the Hermitage in 1763–74, including such masterpieces as Van Dyck's *Family Portrait,* Rembrandt's *Flora,* Jacob van Ruisdael's *Marsh,* Nicolas Lancret's *Ballerina,* and Chardin's *Grace before Dinner,* but it is still a mystery how they got there.

We have a number of descriptions of the picture gallery as it was in the latter half of the eighteenth century. In 1776 the French diplomat Corberon complained in his diary that the paintings were poorly hung and that the galleries flanking the garden were cramped and narrow. In his notes on Russia in 1777–78, Daniel Bernoulli, a member of the Petersburg Academy of Sciences, mentioned his visit to the gallery, which then occupied Vallin de la Mothe's pa-

Bernardino Fungai.
Magnanimity of Scipio Africanus
(panel from a cassone).
Subject from Livy, *History of Rome,*
XXVI, L.
Publius Cornelius Scipio Africanus
(235–183 B.C.) defeated Hannibal
in the Second Punic War.
Tempera and oil on panel.
62 × 166 cm.
Acquired from F. Russov in
Petersburg, 1902.

vilion and the two buildings flanking the Hanging Garden. He too complained that the paintings were "hung at random with different schools jumbled together," but added that "the collection included unexpected treasures and priceless paintings." He also noted that visitors already had a catalogue at their disposal listing no fewer than 2,080 paintings; in 1774 it was published in an edition of only sixty copies.

Overcrowding became even more of a problem at the Hermitage when in 1779 Musin-Pushkin, the Russian ambassador in London, bought most of Sir Robert Walpole's collection from Houghton Hall. This purchase created a sensation, and official attempts

and to commission them to paint new ones. For example, the *Paralytic Helped by His Children,* one of the finest canvases of Jean-Baptiste Greuze, was bought directly from him in 1776, while the *Iron Forge* was purchased from Joseph Wright of Derby in 1775. It was on a special commission from the Russian court that Sir Joshua Reynolds, first president of the Royal Academy, painted his *Infant Hercules Strangling Serpents* (1785), an allegory of young Russia fighting its ene-

Filippino Lippi.
Adoration of the Infant Christ,
c. 1485.
Oil on copper plate, transferred from a panel. Diam. 53 cm. Purchased by Prince V. S. Trubetskoy in Arezzo; later owned by D. M. Mordvinov, bequeathed to A. V. Muravev, sold to P. S. Stroganov in 1859, bequeathed in 1911.

Perugino.
St. Sebastian, c. 1495.
Tempera and oil on panel.
53.5 × 39.5 cm. Purchased from the Marchese N. V. Campanari collection in Rome, 1910; formerly in the Princess Z. A. Volkonskaya collection.

Raphael.
Holy Family (Madonna with Beardless St. Joseph), 1506.
Tempera and oil on canvas, transferred from a panel.
72.5 × 57 cm. Painted in Florence. Purchased from the Crozat collection (Thiers Gallery) in Paris, 1772.

were made to prevent the pictures from leaving the country. As with the Crozat collection, the Walpole pictures were from various sources — a blessing for the Hermitage, with its predominance of Dutch and Flemish art. Among the best items in it were Rubens's *Carters* and *Temple of Janus,* Van Dyck's *Portrait of Elizabeth and Philadelphia Wharton,* Claude Lorrain's *Gulf of Baiae,* and Godfrey Kneller's *Portrait of the Sculptor Grinling Gibbons.*

The last significant purchase made for the Hermitage during the eighteenth century came with the Baudouin collection, bought in Paris in 1781, which consisted of 119 canvases, including nine Rembrandts. By that time the Hermitage had adopted a policy of direct contact with artists, both to buy their works mies. His *Cupid Untying the Zone of Venus* (c. 1788) was acquired in 1792. The largest number of commissions went to the French painters Van Loo, Chardin, and Vigée-Lebrun. It was for the Petersburg Academy of Fine Arts that Chardin painted his *Still Life with the Attributes of the Arts,* which was then brought to Russia by the sculptor Falconet.

A number of French painters and men of letters visited Petersburg and some stayed for quite a while. Diderot himself came as the guest of the imperial government, but the projected visit of Voltaire never took place. Catherine kept up a correspondence with her French friends, however, and after the deaths of Dide-

rot and Voltaire, their large private libraries were bought for the Hermitage.

The royal collections were not the only ones assembled during the eighteenth century, and several of the private collections in Russia contained wonderful works of art. The most famous of these private galleries were those of Ivan Shuvalov, Aleksandr Beloselsky, Aleksandr Stroganov, Nikolai Yusupov, and the Sheremetev family. Many of these works of art eventually found their way to the Hermitage, while the rest were distributed among other museums in the Soviet Union. For example, Simone Martini's *Madonna* and Filippino Lippi's *Adoration of the Infant Christ*

Raphael.
Madonna and Child (the *Connestabile Madonna*), late 1502 to early 1503. Tempera on canvas, transferred from a panel. 17.5 × 18 cm. The frame was probably executed after Raphael's drawing. Painted for Count Alfano di Diamante. Purchased from Count Connestabile of Perugia in 1870; in the Winter Palace until transferred to the Hermitage in 1881.

Leonardo da Vinci.
Madonna with a Flower (the *Benois Madonna*), begun in 1478.
Oil on canvas, transferred from a panel. 49.5 × 31.5 cm, with rounded top.
Acquired from the Benois collection in Petrograd, 1914; formerly in the Sapozhnikov collection in Astrakhan.

Leonardo da Vinci.
Madonna and Child (the *Madonna Litta*). Begun in the late 1470s, probably finished c. 1490–91.
Tempera on canvas, transferred from a panel. 42 × 33 cm.
Purchased from the Duke of Litta's collection in Milan, 1866.

1. Cesare da Sesto.
Holy Family with St. Catherine.
Oil on canvas, transferred from
a panel. 89 × 71 cm.
Acquired between 1763 and 1774.

2. Francesco Melzi.
Portrait of a Woman, c. 1520.
Oil on canvas, transferred from
a panel. 76 × 63 cm.
In the Duke of Orleans collection,
eighteenth century; purchased when
the collection of William II of
the Netherlands was auctioned in
The Hague in 1850.

reached the Hermitage from S.G. Stroganov's collection in Rome in 1911.

As soon as the Felten building was completed in 1787, the second floor of it was taken over by a picture gallery, a detailed account of which was given in Johann Georgi's book *Description of St. Petersburg* (published in 1794), with a list of the paintings to be found in each room. By this time the pictures were hung more systematically, if very close together, occupying all the wall space in the Vallin de la Mothe pavilion, the two galleries flanking the garden, and two suites of rooms in the Felten building. There were also displays of drawings, sculpture, porcelain, and jewelry.

intended for displaying large paintings.

The drawings done by Friedenreich in 1839–41 give us a good idea of what the interiors of the Hermitage were like from the turn of the century until the construction of the New Hermitage, which began in 1842. These drawings come down to us in the dry style of engraving, but they are accurate and informative.

Another way of following the growth of the gallery during the second half of the eighteenth century is by looking at its catalogues. Printed in French in 1774, the first of these contained, as we have said, 2,080 entries. In the Hermitage archives we can find the second, handwritten catalogue, completed in 1783

3. Lorenzo Costa.
Portrait of a Woman, early 1500s.
Tempera and oil on canvas.
57 × 44 cm.
Formerly in the Maria Nikolaevna
collection in Florence; from the
Kochubei collection in Petrograd,
acquired through the State Museum
Depository in 1921.

At this time the billiard room was still situated in the gallery, while the Hermitage pavilion was seeing its last days as a private retreat. On the empress's orders, within the year it was transformed into a drawing room, and the dumbwaiters were dismantled. At the same time a gallery reproducing the Raphael Loggias in the Vatican was constructed at the southeast corner of the Felten building, along with two suites of rooms and listing 2,658 pictures, while by 1797, to judge from an inventory drawn up by a special commission after the death of Catherine, the paintings in the imperial palaces numbered 3,996.

Under Paul I some of the Hermitage paintings were removed to the Castle of Michael (Inzhenerny) in Petersburg, as well as to the Pavlovsk and Gatchina palaces, but all these came back to the Hermitage in due time. Meanwhile, in the last decade of the eighteenth century and the first years of the nineteenth, the museum was acquiring individual paintings, among them one of the finest works of Rubens, *The Union of Earth and Water.*

At the very end of the eighteenth century the museum acquired a staff of experts. The first curator, L. Pfandzelt, was succeeded in 1797 by Franz Labensky, who worked for the museum for over fifty years. It was Labensky who arranged the pictures in proper order, described them and attributed them correctly, and at the same time made new acquisitions. During a visit to Paris in 1808 he bought Caravaggio's celebrated *Lute Player* from the Giustiniani Gallery, while in 1810 he acquired Pieter de Hooch's *Mistress and Maid.* The director of the Louvre at that time, Baron Dominique Vivant Denon, also helped enlarge the Hermitage collection, in accordance with the long-

4. Pontormo (Jacopo Carucci). *Madonna and Child with St. Joseph and John the Baptist,* late 1521 to early 1522. Oil on canvas. 120 × 98.5 cm. The figures of St. Joseph and John the Baptist on either side were added later by the artist. From the Countess Mordvinova collection in Petrograd, acquired through the State Museum Depository in 1923.

5. Francesco Primaticcio. *Holy Family with Saint Elizabeth and John the Baptist.* Oil on slate. 43.5 × 31 cm. Purchased from the Crozat collection (Thiers Gallery) in Paris, 1772.

6. Parmigianino. *Entombment,* c. 1523. Subject from Matthew 27: 57–61; Mark 15: 42–47; Luke 23: 50–56; John 19: 38–42. Oil on canvas, transferred from a panel. 32 × 26.5 cm. Purchased with the Walpole collection from Houghton Hall, England, 1779.

Palma Vecchio.
Portrait of a Man,
between 1512 and 1515.
Oil on canvas. 93.5 × 72 cm.
Acquired from the Golitsyn Museum
in Moscow, 1886.

Titian.
Mary Magdalene Penitent, c. 1560.
Oil on canvas. 118 × 97 cm.
Purchased from the Barbarigo
collection in Venice, 1850.

Titian.
St. Sebastian, c. 1570.
Subject from the *Golden Legend,* XXIII.
Oil on canvas. 210 × 115 cm.
Purchased from the Barbarigo
collection in Venice, 1850.

Lorenzo Lotto.
Portrait of a Young Man, c. 1503.
Oil on canvas, transferred from
a panel. 48 × 38 cm.
Acquired from the Tronchin
collection in Geneva, 1770;
formerly in the Sagredo Palace,
Venice.

Domenico Capriola.
Portrait of a Man, 1512.
Oil on canvas. 117 × 85 cm.
For many years thought to be
Giorgione's self-portrait.
In the Muzelli collection in
Verona, seventeenth century;
purchased from the Crozat
collection (Thiers Gallery)
in Paris, 1772.

Paolo Veronese.
Portrait of a Man, c. 1570.
Oil on canvas. 63 × 50.5 cm.
Purchased from the Barbarigo
collection in Venice, 1850.

established links between the two museums.

Early in the nineteenth century the rooms of the Hermitage were thoroughly rearranged and the first statute of the museum was published, dividing it into five departments. The second of these listed was "the picture gallery, collection of curios, and objects in bronze and marble." A small school of restoration was also set up, with four painters studying under the guidance of Aleksandr Mitrokhin.

The activities of the Hermitage were brought to a halt by the War of 1812. In early September, following Napoleon's invasion of Russia, the museum received orders to evacuate the exhibits in secret. This was carried out so clandestinely that today only the court registers contain any information about the evacuation, or the return of the exhibits in 1813.

In 1814 the Hermitage acquired 118 paintings from Malmaison, the property of Napoleon's ex-wife Josephine. These included some superb works by Flemish, Dutch, and French artists, some of which Napoleon had stolen from various countries as spoils of war. David Teniers's *Guardhouse,* Paulus Potter's *Farm,* and Gerard Ter Borch's *Glass of Lemonade* were among the pictures so acquired. In 1829 more pictures from the same gallery were bought from Josephine's daughter, the Duchess of Saint-Leu.

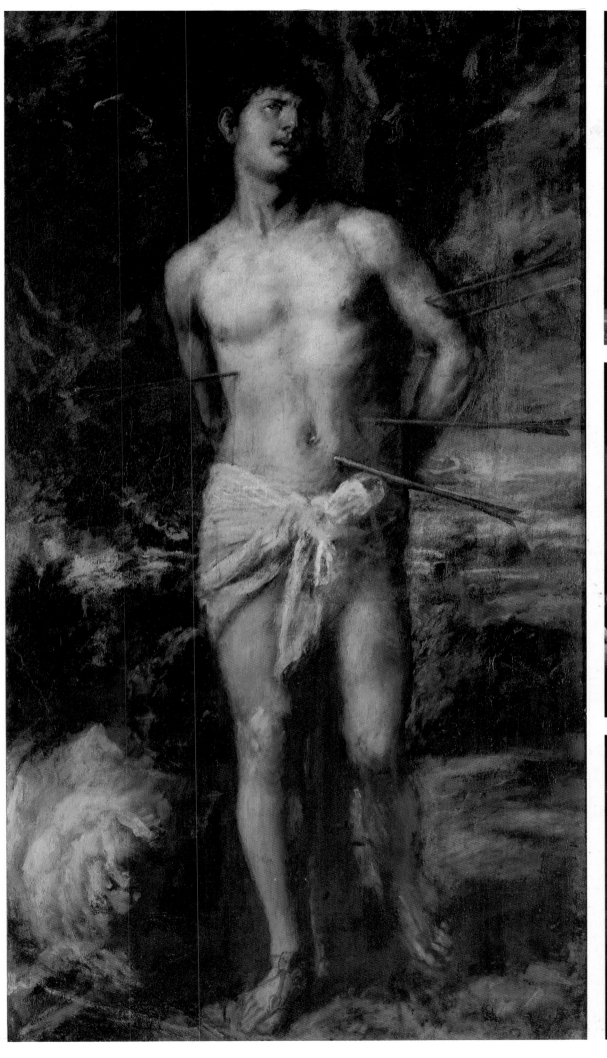

The museum's collection of Spanish paintings was greatly enlarged by acquisitions made in Amsterdam in 1814–15 from the well-known collector Coesvelt. These included the *Portrait of Olivares* by Velázquez, the *Portrait of Don Diego de Villamayor* by Juan Pantoja de la Cruz, and Antonio Pereda's *Still Life.* This nucleus was added to in 1834 by the purchase of works from the collections of Gessler, the Russian consul general in Cádiz, and Paez de la Cadeña, the Spanish ambassador to Russia.

To commemorate the War of 1812, a portrait gallery of the Russian military leaders was set up in the Winter Palace, and Carlo Rossi was commissioned to

design a special hall for it. It was made in imitation of the Windsor Castle gallery containing portraits of the heroes of Waterloo painted by Lawrence. The English artist George Dawe was commissioned to execute the portraits, of which the 1812 Gallery now houses no fewer than 329, done by Dawe and his Russian assistants Golike and Polyakov.

In 1837 a terrible fire all but devastated the Winter Palace, and the Hermitage was saved only at enormous cost and effort by demolishing passages and bricking up doors and windows. The Winter Palace was swiftly reconstructed, but this work distracted the court administration from the problem of the Hermitage, which was in dire need of space, especially since the ground floor of the Felten building had been handed over to the Council of State in 1828. It now became clear that the museum required a whole new

Giorgione (Giorgio da Castelfranco). *Judith.*
Subject from the apocryphal Book of Judith 1:14.
Oil on canvas, transferred from a panel. 144 × 66.5 cm.
Purchased from the Crozat collection (Thiers Gallery) in Paris, 1772.

Paolo Veronese. *Conversion of Saul,* c. 1570.
Subject from Acts 9: 17–20. Oil on canvas. 191 × 329 cm.
Acquired between 1774 and 1783;
in the Gatchina Palace since the early nineteenth century;
returned to the Hermitage in 1920.

Paolo Veronese. *Pietà,* between 1576 and 1582.
Oil on canvas. 147 × 111.5 cm.
Painted for the church of Santi Giovanni e Paolo in Venice.
Purchased from the Crozat collection (Thiers Gallery) in Paris, 1772.

building. This was completed in 1851 and became known as the New Hermitage. The appearance of the new exhibition halls and the pictures displayed in them is accurately recorded in the watercolors done in

123

ITALIAN, *17th century*

1. Giovanni Battista Caracciolo (Battistello). *Christ and Caiaphas.* Oil on canvas. 73 × 103 cm. Purchased from the Brühl collection in Dresden, 1769.

2. Mattia Preti. *Concert,* c. 1630. Oil on canvas. 110 × 147 cm. Purchased from the Crozat collection (Thiers Gallery) in Paris, 1772.

3. Caravaggio. *Lute Player,* c. 1595. Oil on canvas. 94 × 119 cm. Purchased at a Paris auction in 1808.

4. Guido Reni. *Joseph with the Child,* c. 1620. Oil on canvas. 126 × 101 cm. Purchased at an auction in The Hague in 1850.

5. Domenico Fetti. *Portrait of an Actor,* early 1620s. Oil on canvas. 105.5 × 81 cm. Purchased from the Crozat collection (Thiers Gallery) in Paris, 1772.

6. Bernardo Strozzi. *Healing of Tobit,* c. 1635. Oil on canvas. 158 × 223.5 cm. Acquired before 1774.

7. Carlo Maratti. *Portrait of Pope Clement IX.* Clement IX reigned 1667–69. Oil on canvas. 158 × 118.5 cm. Purchased from the Walpole collection in Houghton Hall, England, 1779.

8. Domenico Fetti. *Healing of Tobit,* early 1620s. Oil on panel. 66.7 × 85 cm. Acquired between 1763 and 1774.

6

7

8

125

1852–61 by Eduard Gau and Luigi Premazzi.

The selection and hanging of the pictures was the work of a commission headed by Fëdor Bruni, who had been curator of the gallery since 1849. The works were divided into three groups: those to be displayed at the Hermitage, those to be transferred to other royal palaces, and those to be sold. As a result, 1,219 paintings were sold at auction, though some of them later returned to the Hermitage.

Meanwhile purchases continued and the Hermitage collection grew. In 1850 several Titians were bought in Venice, including *Mary Magdalene Penitent* and *St. Sebastian.* At the same time, when the collec-

ITALIAN
18th century

Alessandro Magnasco.
Resting Highwaymen. From the series probably painted c. 1710. Architecture in the background painted by C. Spero.
Oil on canvas. 112 × 162 cm.
From the Shuvalov collection; transferred from the Academy of Fine Arts in 1922.

Salvator Rosa.
Coastal Scene with Robbers.
Oil on canvas. 52.5 × 91.5 cm.
Purchased from the François de Bourbon-Conti collection in Paris, 1772.

Giuseppe Maria Crespi.
Scene in a Wine Cellar, c. 1710.
Oil on canvas. 52.5 × 42 cm.
Purchased in Paris with the help of Louvre director Dominique Vivant Denon in 1810;
in the Peterhof Palace until 1921.

Vittore Ghislandi.
Portrait of a Boy, 1732 (?).
Oil on canvas. 57 × 52 cm.
Painted in Florence for Marchese Andrea Gerini. From the Kochubei collection in Petrograd; acquired through the State Museum Depository in 1921.

Giovanni Battista Tiepolo.
Maecenas Presenting the Liberal Arts to Augustus, c. 1745.
Oil on canvas. 69.5 × 89 cm.
Commissioned by Count Francesco Algarotti of Venice to eulogize Augustus III of Poland.
Purchased from the Brühl collection in Dresden, 1769;
in the Gatchina Palace, 1797–1882.

126

tion of King William II of the Netherlands was sold at auction, Bruni acquired some very fine pictures, in particular Guido Reni's *Joseph with the Child.* When the Marshal Soult collection was put up at auction in Paris in 1852, he bought Zurbarán's *St. Lawrence.*

In the New Hermitage twenty-one exhibition halls on the second floor were allotted to the picture gallery. The paintings were hung mostly according to national schools, but without any strict order. The new exhibition raised the problem of issuing a catalogue and achieving some order in the storerooms. The inventory completed in 1859 became the basic catalogue to which all subsequent acquisitions were

the smaller adjoining rooms. A separate room was devoted to Russian painters, including Karl Bryulov's *Last Day of Pompeii* and Fëdor Bruni's *Copper Serpent.* All seventy-two paintings of the Russian school were transferred in 1898 to the Russian Museum.

In 1863 Stepan Gedeonov became the first director of the Hermitage, and thanks to him many other outstanding works were bought abroad. In Milan in 1866, for example, Leonardo da Vinci's *Madonna and Child* was bought from the Duke of Litta, whose relatives served at the Russian imperial court. In 1870 one of Raphael's earliest works, the *Madonna and Child,* was bought from Count Connestabile of Perugia; it

added.

The arrangement of the paintings was completed in 1860–61 and remained more or less unchanged until 1914. Large halls were reserved for the works of great painters such as Rembrandt, Rubens, and Van Dyck, while schools of lesser painters were represented in

had been painted about 1500 for Count Alfano di Diamante.

The year 1882 saw the purchase in Florence of a fresco by Fra Angelico, the *Madonna and Child with St. Dominic and St. Thomas Aquinas,* which came from the refectory of the monastery of San Domenico at

Giuseppe Maria Crespi.
Self-portrait, c. 1700.
Oil on canvas. 60.5 × 50 cm (oval).
Purchased from the Baudouin collection
in Paris, 1781.

Francesco Guardi.
View of a Town.
Oil on panel. 52 × 34.5 cm.
Acquired from the Golitsyn Museum
in Moscow, 1886.

Bernardo Bellotto.
*Pirna from the Right Bank
of the Elbe*, between 1747 and 1755.
Oil on canvas. 133.5 × 237.5 cm.
From a series of views of Dresden
and Pirna commissioned by Count
Heinrich von Brühl, minister of
King Augustus III of Saxony.
Purchased from the Brühl collection
in Dresden, 1769; in the Gatchina
Palace since the late nineteenth
century; returned to the Hermitage
in 1920.

Canaletto.
Reception of the French Ambassador in Venice, 1740s.
Count Geurgie, the ambassador, made his visit in 1724. The scene takes place on the embankment near the Doges' Palace.
Oil on canvas. 181 × 259.5 cm.
Acquired between 1763 and 1774.

Francesco Guardi.
View of the Island of San Giorgio Maggiore in Venice.
Oil on canvas. 44 × 60 cm.
Transferred from the Moscow Museum of Modern Western Art in 1927.

Fiesole. In the same year the number of Hermitage paintings was increased by numerous works from the Peterhof and Gatchina palaces, while in 1886 a further seventy-three pictures reached the Hermitage from the Golitsyn collection in Moscow, which had been assembled in the second half of the eighteenth century.

In 1914 Leonardo's wonderful early work *Madonna with a Flower* was bought from Maria Benois (née Sapozhnikov). Legend has it that this painting, sometimes known as the *Benois Madonna,* was bought from a wandering minstrel in Astrakhan, though in point of fact it came from General Korsakov's collection. After the 1917 Revolution responsibility for the

nation's art treasures was entrusted to the State Museum Depository, which distributed works of art among the various museums in the country. In this way the Hermitage came into possession of many paintings formerly in private collections, which filled a number of gaps, especially in works of the nineteenth century.

Continually growing, the gallery came to occupy the entire second floor of the New Hermitage. In 1931 it was extended to include the suite of rooms in the Winter Palace overlooking Palace Square. After the Second World War the exhibition halls were restored. Fortunately, no works of art had been de-

stroyed or damaged during the conflict.

In 1948 the museum received about half the collection of the Moscow Museum of Modern Western Art, formed around Sergei Shchukin's and Ivan Morozov's exceptional collections of late-nineteenth- and early-twentieth-century French paintings. These two collectors were on friendly terms with the painters of the time and had bought the works of unrecognized artists who have since become world-famous. In this way the Hermitage came to possess paintings by Monet, Sisley, Renoir, Pissarro, Degas, Cézanne, Van Gogh, Gauguin, Bonnard, Matisse, Marquet, Derain, and Picasso, now exhibited on the third floor of the Win-

FLEMISH
17th century

1. Adriaen Brouwer. *Scene in a Tavern.*
Oil on panel. 25 × 33.5 cm.
Acquired from the Tronchin collection in Geneva, 1770.

2. Jan Bruegel the Elder
(called "Velvet Bruegel"). *Village Street.*
Oil on copper plate. 25.5 × 38 cm.
Purchased from the Brühl collection in Dresden, 1769.

3. Anthony Van Dyck. *Portrait,* c. 1623.
Oil on canvas. 104 × 86 cm.
Purchased from the Crozat collection
(Thiers Gallery) in Paris, 1772.

4. Anthony Van Dyck. *Self-Portrait,* c. 1630.
Oil on canvas. 116.5 × 93.5 cm.
Purchased from the Crozat collection
(Thiers Gallery) in Paris, 1772.

5. Anthony Van Dyck. *Court Ladies Anne Dalkit, Countess Morton (?), and Anne Kerk,* late 1630s.
Oil on canvas. 131.5 × 150.6 cm.
Acquired between 1763 and 1774.

5

Peter Paul Rubens.
Coronation of the Queen,
between 1622 and 1625.
The coronation of Marie de Médicis
in the cathedral of Saint-Denis in
Paris in 1610.
Oil on panel. 49 × 63 cm.
The first sketch for a painting
in the series, "The Life of Queen
Marie de Médicis of France."
Painted on the Queen's commission
for the Luxembourg Palace gallery
in Paris. Acquired before 1774.

Peter Paul Rubens.
Carters, 1620.
Oil on canvas, transferred from
a panel. 86 × 126.5 cm.
Purchased with the Walpole
collection in Houghton Hall,
England, 1779.

Peter Paul Rubens.
Feast at the House of Simon the Pharisee, between 1618 and 1620.
Subject from Luke 7: 36–38.
Oil on canvas, transferred from a panel. 189 × 254.5 cm.
The heads of three Apostles on Christ's right were painted by Van Dyck.
Purchased with the Walpole collection in Houghton Hall, England, 1779.

Peter Paul Rubens.
Portrait of a Lady-in-waiting of the Infanta Isabella, c. 1625.
Possibly a posthumous portrait of Rubens's eldest daughter, Clara Serena (1611–23).
Oil on panel. 64 × 48 cm.
Purchased from the Crozat collection (Thiers Gallery) in Paris, 1772.

Peter Paul Rubens.
Perseus and Andromeda, early 1620s.
Subject from Ovid's *Metamorphoses,* IV, 668–764.
Oil on canvas, transferred from a panel. 99.5 × 139 cm.
Purchased from the Brühl collection in Dresden, 1769.

David Teniers the Younger.
Guardhouse, 1642.
Oil on panel. 69 × 103 cm.
Purchased from the ex-Empress Josephine's collection
at Malmaison, near Paris, in 1814; formerly in
the collection of the Landgrave of Hesse-Cassel,
until seized by Napoleon in 1806.

Peeter Gysels.
Garden.
Oil on copper plate. 52.5 × 64.5 cm.
Purchased from the Cobentzl collection in Brussels,
1768.

Jacob Jordaens.
The Bean King, c. 1638.
The feast of the Three Kings or Wise Men,
held in the West on January 6.
Oil on canvas, transferred to a new canvas.
157 × 211 cm.
Transferred from the Academy of Fine Arts, 1922.

Frans Snyders.
Fruit Shop.
Oil on canvas. 206 × 342 cm.
Purchased with the Walpole collection in
Houghton Hall, England, 1779.

ter Palace. Among purchases of the last twenty-five years we should mention works by Stanzione and Guttuso (Italy); Teniers and van Ostade (Belgium and Holland); Goya (Spain); Friedrich and Grundig (Germany); Bellange, Boudin, Dufy, Vlaminck, Matisse, and Fougeron (France); and Rockwell Kent (U.S.A.).

The Hermitage collection today includes over 7,700 paintings, the best of which are on display, while the storerooms, where works are hung on sliding boards to facilitate viewing, are open to art historians. Most fully represented is French painting from the fifteenth to the early twentieth centuries. There are, for example, no fewer than seventeen canvases by Nicolas Poussin and eleven by Claude Lorrain. But the thirteenth-to-eighteenth-century Italian collection is also very rich, including works by the leading Renaissance masters, among them Fra Angelico, Leonardo da Vinci, Raphael, Titian, and Veronese. There are numerous Flemish and Dutch masterpieces of the fifteenth to eighteenth centuries—twenty-five Rembrandts in particular. There are valuable English works by Gainsborough, Romney, Reynolds, Lawrence, and Wright, and German ones by Lucas Cranach the Elder, Holbein, and Friedrich.

Extensive research into new techniques of restoration has been carried out at the Hermitage, and these

1. Rogier van der Weyden
(Roger de la Pasture).
*St. Luke Drawing a Portrait of
the Virgin*, c. 1435–40.
Based on a fifth-century Christian
legend of Greek origin.
Oil on canvas, transferred from a
panel. 102.5 × 108.5 cm.
The right half of the painting was
purchased from the collection of
William II of the Netherlands in
1850; the left half, from a
Petersburg art dealer in 1884.

methods have yielded excellent results. An X-ray analysis of the *Adoration of the Magi*, formerly thought to be a copy of the Rembrandt original in the Göteborg Museum in Sweden, revealed some basic changes evidently made by the artist himself; it now seems likely that the Hermitage painting is the original and the Göteborg version a copy by a pupil. The same technique applied to Rembrandt's *Danaë* revealed that, in order to intensify the effect of the shower of gold that appears to emanate from deep within the painting, the artist eliminated some of Danaë's glittering jewelry. It has also come to light that Van Dyck's *Portrait of a Man* was painted over a sketch of Cardinal Guido Ben-

tivoglio, and that *Hagar in the Wilderness* by the French painter Charles de Lafosse was executed on a canvas that already bore a finished portrait by another painter. Furthermore, a portrait of Louis XIV in a medallion on Francesco Solimena's *Allegory of Sovereignty* seems to have been painted over later with portraits of other kings.

The removal of old layers of oil has made it possible to see a number of celebrated paintings in a new light. For example, the colors of Giorgione's *Judith* regained all their original beauty after the removal of both the dark varnish applied by antique dealers and several later additions to the composition.

1

2

4

2. Gillis van Coninxloo.
Landscape with a Scene from the Myth of Leto and the Lycians.
The subject from Ovid, *Metamorphoses,* VI, 314–81.
Oil on canvas. 143.5 × 204 cm.
The figures were probably painted by Hendrick de Clerck.
Purchased when the Schubart collection was auctioned in Munich in 1894.

3. Frans Pourbus the Elder.
Portrait of a Man and *Portrait of a Woman.*
Oil on panel.
Each portrait 87 × 78 cm.
Purchased with the Gotzkowski collection in Berlin in 1763.

4. Pieter Bruegel the Younger.
Fair, 1562 (?).
Copy of a work by Pieter Bruegel the Elder; the original has been lost.
Oil on panel. 110 × 164.5 cm.
Acquired through the Leningrad State Purchasing Commission.

Robert Campin
(the Master of
Flémalle).
Holy Trinity and
*Virgin and Child at
the Fireside* (left
and right wings
of a diptych).
Oil on panel.
Each wing
34 × 24.5 cm.
Ornamental painted
framing of a later date.
Bequeathed by
Dmitri Tatishchev in
Petersburg, 1845.

Lucas van Leyden.
Healing of the Blind Man of Jericho
(triptych), 1531.
Subject from Mark 10: 46–52;
Luke 18: 35–43.
Oil on canvas, transferred from a
panel. Central part 115.5 ×
150.5 cm; wings 89 × 33 cm each.
The warrior and the girl on the
wings hold the coat-of-arms of the
donors, Jacob Floriszon van
Monfort of Leyden and his wife.
Purchased from the Crozat
collection (Thiers Gallery)
in Paris, 1772.

Lucas van Leyden.
*Healing of the Blind Man of
Jericho,* 1531.
Detail.

Jan Gossaert (Mabuse).
Deposition (central panel of
a triptych), 1521.
Subject from John 19: 38–40.
Oil on canvas, transferred from a
panel. 141 × 106.5 cm.
Painted for a chapel of the church
of St. Augustine in Bruges.
Purchased when the collection of
William II of the Netherlands was
auctioned at The Hague in 1850.

141

3

1

4

2

5

1. Pieter Claesz.
Pipes and Brazier, 1636.
Oil on panel. 49 × 63.5 cm.
From the Argutinsky-Dolgorukov
collection in Petrograd, acquired
through the State Museum
Depository, 1921.

2. Pieter Claesz.
Breakfast with Ham, 1647.
Oil on panel. 40 × 61 cm.
Purchased from V. P. Kostromitinova
in Petersburg, 1895.

3. Dirck van Baburen.
Concert, c. 1623.
Oil on canvas. 99 × 130 cm.
Purchased with the Gotzkowski
collection in Berlin, 1763.

4. Willem Kalf.
Dessert.
Oil on canvas. 105 × 87.5 cm.
Purchased from the P. P. Semënov-
Tien-Shansky collection, 1915.

5. Abraham Bloemaert.
Landscape with Tobias and the Angel.
Subject from the apocryphal
Book of Tobit 6: 1–18.
Oil on canvas. 139 × 107.5 cm.
Transferred from the Petrograd
Society for Encouraging the Arts in
1919; formerly in the Marble Palace.

6. Adriaen van Ostade.
Scuffle, 1637.
Oil on panel. 25 × 33.5 cm.
In the Peterhof Palace of Mon
Plaisir since 1716; transferred to
the Hermitage in 1882.

7. Paulus Potter.
Farm, 1649.
Oil on panel. 81 × 115.5 cm.
Purchased from the ex-Empress
Josephine's collection at Malmaison,
near Paris, in 1814.

8. Jacob van Ruisdael.
Marsh, c. 1660.
Oil on canvas. 72.5 × 99 cm.
Acquired between 1763 and 1774.

9. Aert de Gelder.
*Self-Portrait with Rembrandt's
Etching.*
Oil on canvas. 79 × 64 cm.
Acquired in 1895 from the
Łazienki Palace in Warsaw.

10. Philips Wouwerman.
View of a Haarlem Suburb.
Oil on canvas. 76 × 67 cm.
Purchased from the Brühl
collection in Dresden, 1769.

11. Gerard (Gerrit) Dou.
Astronomer, c. 1628.
Oil on panel. 38.5 × 31 cm.
Purchased from the E. K. Lipgart
collection in Petersburg, 1906.

Frans van Mieris the Elder.
Breakfast with Oysters, 1659.
Oil on panel. 44.5 × 34.5 cm (rounded top).
Purchased from the Brühl collection in Dresden, 1769.

Gabriel Metsu.
Breakfast, c. 1660.
Oil on panel.
56 × 42 cm.
Purchased from the ex-Empress Josephine's collection at Malmaison, near Paris, in 1814.

Willem Claesz Heda.
Breakfast with Lobster, 1648.
Oil on canvas.
118 × 118 cm.
Transferred from the State Museum Depository, 1920.

Willem Cornelisz Duyster.
Officers Playing Backgammon, c. 1630.
Oil on panel. 31.5 × 42.5 cm (oval).
Acquired between 1781 and 1785.

1. Rembrandt.
Holy Family, 1645.
Oil on canvas. 117 × 91 cm.
Purchased from the Crozat
collection (Thiers Gallery)
in Paris, 1772.

2. Rembrandt.
Young Woman with Earrings, 1657.
Oil on panel, 39.5 × 32.5 cm.
Purchased from the Baudouin
collection in Paris, 1781.

3. Rembrandt.
Danaë, 1636.
Oil on canvas. 185 × 202.5 cm.
Purchased from the Crozat
collection (Thiers Gallery)
in Paris, 1772.

4. Rembrandt.
David's Farewell to Jonathan, 1642.
From 1 Samuel 20: 41–42.
Oil on panel. 73 × 61.5 cm.
Purchased on Peter the Great's
orders from the Jan van Buyningen
collection in Amsterdam in 1716;
in the Peterhof Palace of
Mon Plaisir until 1882, when
transferred to the Hermitage.

1

2

3

Rembrandt f. 1642

1. Frans Hals.
Portrait of a Man, before 1660.
Oil on canvas. 84.5 × 67 cm.
Acquired between 1763 and 1774.

2. Frans Hals.
*Portrait of a Young Man with
a Glove,* c. 1650.
Oil on canvas. 80 × 66.5 cm
(pieces added on top and sides).
Purchased with the Gotzkowski
collection in Berlin, 1763.

3. Gerard Ter Borch.
Portrait of Katarina van Luynink.
Oil on canvas. 80 × 59 cm.
From the Kushelev collection;
transferred from the Academy of
Fine Arts, 1922.

4. Jan Steen.
Smoker, early 1650s.
Oil on panel. 38 × 32 cm
(including the added piece).
Purchased with the Gotzkowski
collection in Berlin, 1763.

5. Gerard Ter Borch.
Glass of Lemonade.
Oil on canvas, transferred from
a panel. 67 × 54 cm.
Purchased from the ex-Empress
Josephine's collection at Malmaison,
near Paris, in 1814.

6. Jacob van Ruisdael.
*Peasant Cottages in a
Dune Landscape,* 1647.
Oil on panel. 52.5 × 67 cm.
Purchased from the Baudouin
collection in Paris, 1781.

7. Jan van Goyen.
Winter Landscape near the Hague,
1645.
Oil on panel. 52 × 70 cm.
Acquired before 1797.

148

8

9

10

8. Gerard van Honthorst.
Woman Playing the Lute, 1624.
Oil on canvas. 84 × 66.5 cm.
Purchased with the Gotzkowski collection
in Berlin, 1763.

9. Jan Hackaert. *Deer Hunt.*
Oil on canvas. 120.5 × 101.5 cm.
Figures painted by Johannes Lingelbach.
Acquired through the State Museum
Depository from the Sapegi collection
in Grodno, 1932.

10. Vincent van Gogh.
Thatched Cottages, 1890.
Oil on canvas. 60 × 73 cm.
From the Morozov collection in Moscow;
transferred from the
Museum of Modern Western Art, 1948.

11. Pieter de Hooch.
Mistress and Maid, c. 1660.
Oil on canvas. 53 × 42 cm.
Purchased from the Paris art dealer
Lafontaine in 1810.

11

149

Lucas Cranach the Elder.
*Virgin and Child
under an Apple Tree.*
Oil on canvas,
transferred from a panel.
87 × 59 cm.
Acquired before 1859.

1

2

3

4

5

1. Joseph Wright of Derby.
Iron Forge, 1773.
Oil on canvas. 105 × 140 cm.
Purchased from the artist,
late 1774 to early 1775.

2. Godfrey Kneller.
*Portrait of the Sculptor
Grinling Gibbons,* before 1690.
Grinling Gibbons (1648–1720)
was a noted English sculptor and
wood carver.
Oil on canvas. 125 × 90 cm.
Purchased from the Walpole
collection in Houghton Hall,
England, 1779.

3. Thomas Gainsborough.
Portrait of a Lady in Blue,
late 1770s.
Oil on canvas. 76 × 64 cm.
A. Z. Khitrovo donation, 1912–16.

4. George Dawe.
Portrait of P. M. Volkonsky,
before 1823.
Pëtr Mikhailovich Volkonsky,
prince and lieutenant general
(1776–1852).
Oil on canvas. 70 × 62.5 cm.
Painted for the Winter Palace's
Gallery of the War of 1812,
commemorating Russia's victory.
Designed by Carlo Rossi, the
gallery displays portraits of
Russian generals who participated
in the campaigns of 1812–14.

5. Joshua Reynolds.
Cupid Untying the Zone of Venus
(unfinished), 1788.
Oil on canvas. 127.5 × 101 cm.
Acquired from the G. A. Potemkin
collection, 1792.

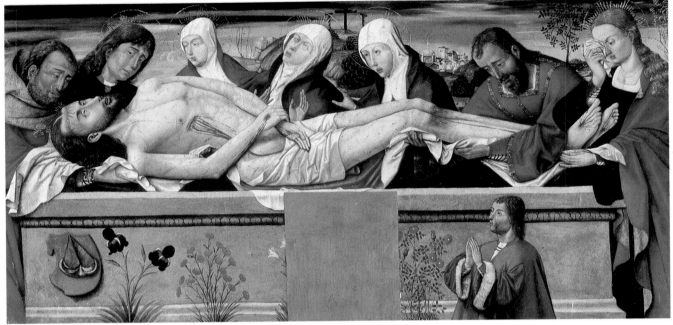

SPANISH

Juan Pantoja de la Cruz.
Portrait of Don Diego de Villamayor,
1605.
Oil on canvas. 89 × 71 cm.
Purchased with the Coesvelt
collection in Amsterdam, 1814; in
the Tsarskoe Selo Arsenal, 1833–88.

Anonymous artist of the
Castilian School.
Entombment, second half of
fifteenth century.
Subject from Matthew 27: 57–61;
Mark 15: 42–47; Luke 23: 50–56;
John 19: 38–42.
Tempera and oil on panel.
94 × 182 cm. (The lower part of
the center panel is lost.)
Acquired from a Leningrad antique
dealer in 1933.

Diego Velázquez.
Lunch, c. 1617–18.
Oil on canvas. 108.5 × 102 cm.
Acquired between 1763 and 1774
from an unknown collection.

El Greco.
Peter and Paul,
between 1587 and 1592.
Subject from the *Golden Legend,*
LXXXIX.
Oil on canvas. 121.5 × 105 cm.
Donated by P. P. Durnovo, 1911.

153

1. Luis de Morales.
Mater Dolorosa.
Oil on panel. 82.5 × 58 cm.
Purchased with the Coesvelt
collection in Amsterdam, 1814.

2. Francisco de Zurbarán.
Girlhood of the Virgin, c. 1660.
Subject from the *Golden Legend,*
CXXIX, 1.
Oil on canvas. 73.5 × 53.5 cm.
Purchased with the Coesvelt
collection in Amsterdam, 1814.

3. José Ribera.
Saints Sebastian and Irene, 1628.
Oil on canvas. 156 × 188 cm.
Purchased from the collection of
the Duchess of Saint-Leu in 1829;
formerly in the Malmaison
collection, near Paris.

4, 5. Antonio Pereda.
Still Life.
Oil on canvas. 80 × 94 cm.
Purchased with the Coesvelt
collection in Amsterdam, 1814.

6. Francisco Ribalta.
Portrait of Lope de Vega.
Oil on canvas. 65.5 × 50 cm.
Purchased with the Coesvelt
collection in Amsterdam, 1814.

7. Bartolomé Estebán Murillo.
Boy with a Dog, c. 1650.
Oil on canvas. 74 × 60 cm.
Purchased from the Choiseul
collection in Paris, 1772.

8. Francisco de Goya.
*Portrait of the Actress
Antonia Zárate,* c. 1811.
Antonia Zárate (1775–1811) was
a Madrid actress.
Oil on canvas. 71 × 58 cm.
Donated by Armand Hammer of
the United States, 1972.

1

2

3

4

5 4206

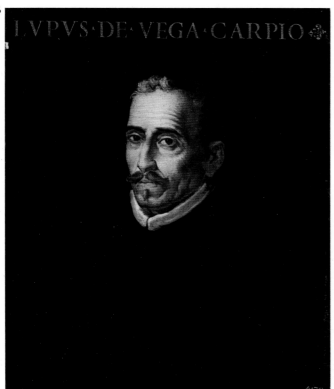

6

4170

7

8

Corneille de Lyon.
Portrait of a Woman, c. 1530–40.
Oil on panel. 20 × 15.5 cm.
Transferred from the Shuvalov
house-museum in Leningrad, 1925.

Anonymous French artist of
the sixteenth century.
Portrait of a Man, late 1560s.
Oil on panel. 48.5 × 32 cm.
Purchased with the Crozat
collection (Thiers Gallery) in Paris,
1772.

Nicolas de Largillière.
*Municipal Council Meeting at the
Paris City Hall,* c. 1687.
Sketch for a painting that was
made in 1687 for a room in the
Paris City Hall; the painting was
subsequently destroyed by fire.
Oil on canvas. 68 × 101 cm.
Purchased from the Crozat
collection (Thiers Gallery) in Paris,
1772.

Claude Lorrain (Claude Gellée). *Evening,* 1663.
Oil on canvas. 116 × 153.5 cm.
From the "Times of Day" series. Figures presumably
painted by the Italian artist F. Lauri (1623–94).
Purchased from the ex-Empress Josephine's collection
at Malmaison, near Paris, in 1814; formerly in the
Landgrave of Hesse-Cassel's collection.

Claude Lorrain (Claude Gellée). *Noon,* 1651 (or 1661).
Oil on canvas. 113 × 157 cm.
Also from the "Times of Day" series.

Claude Lorrain (Claude Gellée). *Gulf of Baiae,* c. 1650.
Oil on canvas. 99.5 × 125 cm.
Purchased from the Walpole collection in Houghton Hall,
England, 1779.

157

1. Nicolas Poussin.
Tancred and Erminia, c. 1630.
Subject from Torquato Tasso's
Jerusalem Delivered, XIX.
Oil on canvas. 98.5 × 146.5 cm.
Purchased at a Paris auction of
the artist J. A. Aved's collection,
1766.

2. Nicolas Poussin.
*Battle of the Israelites with
the Amalekites*, c. 1625.
Subject from Exodus 17: 8–13.
Oil on canvas. 97.5 × 134 cm.
Acquired between 1763 and 1774.

3. Nicolas Poussin.
Landscape with Polyphemus, 1649.
Subject from Ovid's *Metamorphoses*,
XIII, 760–856.
Oil on canvas. 150 × 199 cm.
Purchased from the Marquis
de Conflans's collection in Paris,
1772.

4. Pierre Dumoustier.
Portrait of a Young Man.
Oil on canvas. 32 × 19 cm.
Purchased with the Cobentzl
collection in Brussels, 1768.

3

4

5

6

7

8

5. Nicolas Lancret.
Camargo Dancing.
Marie Anne de Cupis de Camargo
(1710–70) was a well-known French
dancer.
Oil on canvas. 54 × 55 cm.
Acquired between 1763 and 1774.

6. Antoine Watteau.
Actors of the Comédie-Française,
c. 1712.
Group portrait of Comédie-Française
actors, apparently performing
Les Trois cousines by F. C. Dancourt
(1661–1725). On the right is
Pierre le Noir la Thorillière, and
on the left, Christine-Antoinette
Desmares; the young man with a
beret is Phillippe Poisson.
Oil on panel. 20 × 25 cm.
Purchased from the Crozat
collection (Thiers Gallery)
in Paris, 1772. In the Gatchina
Palace since the early nineteenth
century; transferred to the
Hermitage in 1920.

7. Louis Le Nain.
The Milkwoman's Family, c. 1640.
Oil on canvas. 51 × 59 cm.
Acquired between 1763 and 1774.

8. Antoine Watteau.
Savoyard with a Marmot, 1716.
Oil on canvas. 40.5 × 32.5 cm.
From the C. Audran collection in
Paris, acquired before 1774.

FRENCH
18th century

Jean-Baptiste Perronneau.
Boy with a Book, c. 1740.
Oil on canvas. 63 × 52 cm.
Purchased from the A.G. Teplov
collection in Petersburg, 1781.

Jean-Honoré Fragonard.
The Captured Kiss.
Oil on canvas. 47 × 60 cm.
Transferred from the Yusupov palace-
museum in Leningrad, 1925.

François Boucher.
Pastoral Scene.
Oil on canvas. 61 × 75 cm (oval).
The painted area was changed from
oval to irregular in 1856, then
back to oval in 1902.
Acquired between 1763 and 1774.

Jean-Baptiste Chardin.
Grace before Dinner, 1744.
Oil on canvas. 49.5 × 38.4 cm.
Acquired between 1763 and 1774.

Jean-Baptiste Chardin.
Washerwoman.
Oil on canvas. 37.5 × 42.7 cm.
Purchased from the Crozat
collection (Thiers Gallery)
in Paris, 1772.

Jean-Baptiste Chardin.
*Still Life with the Attributes
of the Arts,* 1766.
Oil on canvas. 112 × 140.5 cm.
Painted for the Petersburg Academy
of Fine Arts.
Acquired in 1766; sold at auction
in 1854; reacquired in 1926.

FRENCH
19th and 20th centuries

1. Dominique Ingres.
Count N. D. Gurev, 1821.
Nikolai Gurev (1792–1849) served
as Russian ambassador to The Hague,
Rome, and Naples.
Oil on canvas. 107 × 86 cm.
From the A. N. Naryshkina collection
in Petrograd; transferred through
the State Museum Depository in 1922.

2. Eugène Delacroix.
Arab Saddling His Horse, 1855.
Oil on canvas. 56 × 47 cm.
From the Kushelev collection;
transferred from the Academy of
Fine Arts in 1922.

3. Camille Corot.
Landscape with a Lake, 1860–1873.
Oil on canvas. 53 × 65.5 cm.
Acquired in 1879; transferred
from the Yusupov palace-museum in
Leningrad, 1925.

1

2

3

4

4. Jean-François Millet.
Peasant Women Carrying Firewood, c. 1858.
Oil on canvas. 37.5 × 29.5 cm.
From the Kushelev collection; transferred from the
Academy of Fine Arts in 1922.

5. Camille Pissarro.
Boulevard Montmartre in Paris, 1897.
Oil on canvas. 73 × 92 cm.
From the Ryabushinsky collection in Moscow;
transferred from the Museum of Modern Western Art
in 1948.

6. Théodore Rousseau.
Market in Normandy, c. 1830.
Oil on panel. 29.5 × 38 cm.
From the Kushelev collection; transferred from the
Academy of Fine Arts in 1922.

7. Claude Monet.
Meadows in Giverny, 1888.
Oil on canvas. 92 × 80 cm.
From the Shchukin collection in Moscow;
transferred from the Museum of Modern Western Art
in 1934.

8. Claude Monet.
Haystack in Giverny, 1886.
Oil on canvas. 61 × 81 cm.
From the Shchukin collection in Moscow;
transferred from the Museum of Modern Western Art
in 1931.

5

6

7

8

163

1. Paul Gauguin.
Woman Holding a Mango, 1893.
Oil on canvas. 92 × 73 cm.
From the Morozov collection in
Moscow; transferred from the Museum
of Modern Western Art in 1948.

2. Paul Cézanne.
*Girl at the Piano (Overture
from* Tannhäuser*)*, c. 1868–69.
The sitters were the painter's
mother and elder sister.
Oil on canvas. 57 × 92 cm.
From the Morozov collection in
Moscow; transferred from the Museum
of Modern Western Art in 1948.

3. Maurice Denis.
Martha and Mary, 1896.
Subject from Luke 10: 38–42.
Oil on canvas. 77 × 116 cm.
From the Shchukin collection in
Moscow; transferred from the Museum
of Modern Western Art in 1948.

4. Alfred Sisley.
Villeneuve-la-Garenne on the Seine,
1872.
Oil on canvas. 59 × 80.5 cm.
From the Shchukin collection in
Moscow; transferred from the Museum
of Modern Western Art in 1948.

5. Paul Cézanne.
Still Life with Drapery, c. 1899.
Oil on canvas. 53 × 72 cm.
From the Morozov collection in
Moscow; transferred from the Museum
of Modern Western Art in 1930.

6. Henri Matisse.
Blue Jar and a Lemon, 1897.
Oil on canvas. 39 × 46.5 cm.
From the Morozov collection in
Moscow; transferred from the Museum
of Modern Western Art in 1948.

5

6

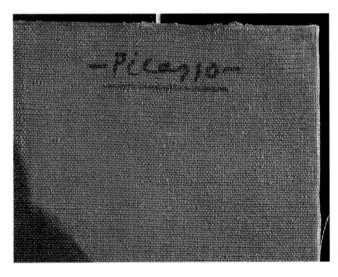

1. Albert Marquet.
View of the Seine and a Monument to Henry IV, c. 1907.
Oil on canvas. 65 × 81 cm.
From the Morozov collection in Moscow; transferred from the Museum of Modern Western Art in 1948.

2. Albert Marquet.
Marina (Naples), 1909.
Oil on canvas. 61.5 × 80 cm.
From the Morozov collection in Moscow; transferred from the Museum of Modern Western Art in 1948.

3. Henri Rousseau.
In a Tropical Forest: A Tiger and a Bull Fighting, 1908 (?).
Oil on canvas. 46 × 55 cm.
From the Shchukin collection in Moscow; transferred from the Museum of Modern Western Art in 1930.

4. André Derain.
The Grove, c. 1912.
Oil on canvas. 116 × 81 cm.
From the Shchukin collection in Moscow; transferred from the Museum of Modern Western Art in 1948.

5. André Derain.
Table and Chairs, c. 1912.
Oil on canvas. 87 × 85.5 cm.
From the Morozov collection in Moscow; transferred from the Museum of Modern Western Art in 1948.

6. Pablo Picasso.
Absinthe Drinker, 1901.
Oil on canvas. 73 × 54 cm.
From the Shchukin collection in Moscow; transferred from the Museum of Modern Western Art in 1948.

Pablo Picasso.
Woman with a Fan (After a Ball),
1908.
Oil on canvas. 150 × 100 cm.
From the Shchukin collection
in Moscow; transferred from the
Museum of Modern Western Art
in 1934.

Henri Matisse.
Family Portrait, 1911.
Oil on canvas. 143 × 194 cm.
From the Shchukin collection in
Moscow; transferred from the Museum
of Modern Western Art in 1948.

Pierre Dumoustier the Elder.
Portrait of Etienne Dumoustier,
c. 1570.
Etienne Dumoustier (1540–1603) was
painted by his elder brother at
the age of twenty-nine.
Black chalk and pastel. 40 × 27 cm.
Purchased from the Cobentzl
collection, 1768.

The Hermitage collection of drawings by old masters is large and of high quality, but unfortunately uneven. There is no lack of work by Italian, French, and Flemish artists of the sixteenth to nineteenth centuries, but drawings by the great Italian masters of the early Renaissance are almost completely lacking. This unevenness can be explained by the sources of the drawings, most of which came with the collections of Count Cobentzl (3,760 drawings in 1768) and Count Heinrich von Brühl (1,706 drawings in 1769). The latter collection, assembled for the most part in Brussels, included about thirty stupendous drawings by Rubens (*Deposition, Mars and Venus, Stoning of St.*

Stephen, and so on), as well as others by Jacob Jordaens and Van Dyck. Outstanding among the Cobentzl collection are the fifteenth- and sixteenth-century French portraits in pencil: 129 drawings by Jean Fouquet, François Clouet, Pierre and Etienne Dumoustier, and others that provide us with a whole gallery of the personalities of the time—kings and queens, courtiers, soldiers, and the common people. This collection is excelled in its field only by the drawings in the Bibliothèque Nationale in Paris and the Musée de Chantilly. The Brühl collection gave the Hermitage some drawings by Italian artists such as Titian and Veronese, and even more by Flemish and Dutch masters (including the remarkable *Winter Landscape* done by Rembrandt on special paper), and others by French artists of the eighteenth century.

Subsequent acquisitions added considerably to individual sections; for example, the late-eighteenth-century purchase of the Julienne collection brought with it an album of 853 drawings by Jacques Callot. In 1920 the museum of the Stieglitz Institute of Crafts gave the Hermitage about nine thousand drawings, which formed the basis of the section of applied arts of the sixteenth to eighteenth centuries. Along with these drawings came some priceless illuminated manuscripts: the *Treatise on Hunting* (1381), a fourteenth-century French book of hours, and a late-fifteenth-century copy of the *Roman de la Rose.* These are kept in the rare books department of the museum's central library.

In 1924 the Academy of Fine Arts gave the Hermitage more than two thousand fifteenth-to-eighteenth-century drawings from the collection made by Ivan Betsky in the second half of the eighteenth century. These included a fine set of drawings by Jean-Baptiste Greuze, who had close links with Russia and painted several works commissioned by the Hermitage.

The museum also has about one hundred drawings by well-known eighteenth-century Italian theatrical designers. But by no means are all of these sketches for the stage; quite a few are free compositions inspired by the sumptuous masques and entertainments given at court and in the homes of the nobility. The artists represented include the Galli Bibiena family, Giuseppe Valeriani, and Pietro Gonzaga, of whom the latter two had connections with Russia. Valeriani came to Petersburg with an Italian theater company in 1742 and stayed on to collaborate with Rastrelli, working on palace interiors in Petersburg itself and at Tsarskoe Selo. Gonzaga came to Petersburg in 1792, when the architect Quarenghi invited him to help work on the emperor's theater, but he also did frescoes and landscaped gardens at the Pavlovsk Palace, skillfully exploiting the colors of autumnal foliage.

Of particular interest are sets of drawings by the architects Giacomo Quarenghi, Charles Cameron, Thomas Jean Thomas de Thomon, Andrei Voronikhin, and others who worked on the palaces on the outskirts of Petersburg. These drawings proved essential when the ruined palaces and parks of Peterhof, Tsarskoe Selo, and Pavlovsk were being restored. Other items of interest are the excellent watercolors of Winter Palace and Hermitage interiors done by Konstantin Ukhtomsky, Eduard Gau, and Luigi Premazzi in 1852–61. The Hermitage also possesses a large and varied collection of engravings, etchings, and lithographs.

The first engravings came to the Winter Palace in 1768 along with other items from the Cobentzl, Brühl, and Walpole collections, as well as the Monetti

and engravings and prints of historical events, battle scenes, and military uniforms. Of special interest are the architectural items, particularly those dealing with ornaments, and the illustrations from printed books. Dmitri Rovinsky's famous collection of Rembrandt's etchings, with impressions showing the successive stages of the work, was a notable addition to this section in 1895.

By 1914 the prints in the Hermitage totaled 360,000. But even this number increased considerably after the October Revolution, thanks to the absorption of the major collections of the Russian Museum, the Stroganov Palace, the Academy of Fine Arts, and

Peter Paul Rubens.
Stoning of St. Stephen, c. 1615.
Black and red chalk, washed with bister and watercolor, with occasional pen touches. 47 × 32.5 cm.
The final version of the central panel of a triptych for the Saint Aman abbey near Valenciennes, France, showing the influence of a composition by the Italian artist Lodovico Chigoli (1559–1613).

Rembrandt.
Village Street, c. 1640–42.
Pen and brown wash partly toned down with white.
17.8 × 33.5 cm.
Acquired before 1797.

collection, bought by Prince Grigori Potemkin. Single sheets were also bought from booksellers in Petersburg—a trade that flourishes in the city today. In 1805 a special room was set aside for the study of engravings, and painters and architects made good use of it. Even before this time it is known that Cameron, Quarenghi, Gonzaga, and Reichel used to haunt the collection of engravings. At the end of the eighteenth century the court architect, Vikenti Brenna, was put in charge of the engravings; the catalogue of them compiled by the curator Labensky listed 44,454 sheets.

During the nineteenth century the Hermitage obtained a large collection of English caricatures; engravings of works by famous painters from various galleries; a vast series of over sixty thousand portraits; landscapes and views of cities and individual buildings;

Carlo Galli Bibiena.
Landscape, eighteenth century.
Pen and brush, wash, India ink, and watercolor. 286 × 440 cm.
Acquired before 1797.

the Stieglitz Institute. By 1941 there were 470,000 engravings, etchings, and lithographs; today, over half a million.

The museum also has some outstanding Western European sculpture from the fifteenth to twentieth centuries. At first, from the time of Peter the Great on, sculpture brought from the West was intended as decoration for the palaces and gardens. Perhaps the museum's first collection was the one bought in England from Lyde Brown in 1787. Along with the ancient statues that so enriched the Antiquities Department came some outstanding Renaissance sculpture, including Michelangelo's *Crouching Boy* and the *Dead*

Boy on a Dolphin by Lorenzetto.

The wonderful figure of the crouching boy, wounded in one leg, may have been a model for the Medici tomb in Florence. The whole attitude of the youth is expressive of the pain he feels, while his resilient bent back reveals the artist's mastery of anat-

omy. The Lorenzetto statue was made for a fountain after a design by the artist's friend Raphael and is inspired by the beautiful legend of the dolphins' kindness toward children.

Many of the eighteenth-century sculptures at the Winter Palace were commissioned by the imperial court or were purchased from artists associated in some way with Russia. For example, it was for Catherine the Great that Jean-Antoine Houdon created his 1781 masterpiece, the statue of Voltaire seated in an armchair, a lively, mocking, and penetrating look on his face. We know from the memoirs of various courtiers that Nicholas I hated Voltaire and referred to the Houdon statue as "the old monkey." Although it was removed from the royal presence, Nicholas kept running into it, until it was eventually locked away in a storeroom in the public library before at last finding its way to the Hermitage.

The museum prides itself on several works by the French sculptor Etienne-Maurice Falconet, who worked in Petersburg from 1766 to 1778 and made the famous equestrian statue of Peter the Great, the *Bronze Horseman,* that stands in Senate Square. On display next to Falconet's statues is a fine portrait of the artist by his pupil Marie-Anne Collot, who also worked in Russia.

When the New Hermitage was opened, Western European sculpture was brought to it from the outlying palaces and gardens. At first these pieces, along with works by Russian sculptors, were placed near the antiquities on the ground floor, but they were then moved to adorn the upper landing of the Grand Staircase and the Gallery of the History of Ancient Painting, so called because its walls bear no fewer than eighty panels by the Munich painter Georg Hiltensperger depicting the lives of artists of antiquity. These sculptures included some fine works by Canova (*Cupid and Psyche, Dancer,* and *Mary Magdalene Penitent*), Thorvaldsen (*Ganymede* and *Portrait of Ostermann-Tolstaya*), Dupré (*Cain* and *Abel*), and Bartolini (*Nymph Bitten by a Scorpion* and *Young Grape Picker*). Another significant addition to the sculpture section was the Aleksandr Bazilevsky collection that came from Paris in 1885, including many works in wood from the Middle Ages and from the Renaissance in Italy, Germany, and the Netherlands.

Fifteenth-century Italian sculpture is represented by works of Andrea della Robbia and Antonio Rossellino; the sixteenth and seventeenth centuries, by a collection of small bronzes (Giambologna, Niccolò Roccatagliata, Alessandro Vittoria) that once belonged to Dmitri Tatishchev. There is also an exceptionally fine collection of seventeenth-century Italian terra cottas that came from the Academy of Fine Arts in 1919. This included some brilliant works by Giovanni Lorenzo Bernini (*Rapture of St. Teresa, Self-Portrait,* and others) and two terra-cotta portraits of a man and wife of the Pamphili family by Alessandro Algardi. The collection of sculptures by Auguste Rodin, displayed in a separate hall, as well as individual works by Constantin Meunier, Aristide Maillol, Henri Matisse, and the Hungarian sculptor Alajos Strobl, all came from private collections or as donations. Matisse's *Foot* (1909–10) was a study for his famous painting *The Dance*.

The Hermitage is renowned for its collection of medieval applied art in the Romanesque and Gothic styles, from the eleventh to the fifteenth centuries. In spite of their fine workmanship, most of these articles made in monasteries are anonymous; not until the end of the thirteenth century, with the spread of urban culture, did artists begin signing their works. The gem of the collection is a gilded silver figure of St. Stephen as a deacon holding the Gospels, the work of a twelfth-century French master. No less beautiful is the so-called Freiburg Cross, a French work of the thirteenth century with exquisitely wrought figures of the Virgin and St. John that have justly been compared with the stone figures of Rheims cathedral. The cross is studded with many colored stones, some of them ancient and bearing the carved figure of Athena.

Much of this medieval applied art, and particularly the church utensils and ornaments, came from the

SCULPTURE

Antonio Rossellino.
Madonna and Child,
mid-fifteenth century.
Marble. 67 × 54 cm.
Acquired in 1914.

Michelangelo Buonarroti.
Crouching Boy.
Marble. Height 54 cm.
Made for the Medici tomb in the church of San Lorenzo in Florence. Purchased with the Lyde Brown collection at Wimbledon in 1787; in the Hermitage since 1851.

Jean-Antoine Houdon.
Voltaire Seated in an Armchair,
1781.
Marble. Height 138 cm.
Commissioned by Catherine the
Great and brought to Tsarskoe Selo
in 1784. In the Hermitage since
the 1820s.

Antonio Canova.
Cupid and Psyche.
Marble. Height 150 cm.
Purchased from the ex-Empress
Josephine's collection at Malmaison,
near Paris, in 1814.

above-mentioned Bazilevsky collection, but even Peter the Great's Kunstkammer contained such works as a fourteenth-century Syrian glass horn with paintings and a Kufic inscription (set in an ornamental silver frame in 1551), and a delicate Gothic reliquary made of silver by the Tallinn master Hans Rissenberg in 1474.

Other applied-art collections include the fifteenth- and sixteenth-century Limoges *champlevé* enamels; the carved ivory from Italy, France, Germany, and the Netherlands of the fifteenth to eighteenth centuries; and silverware of the sixteenth to eighteenth centuries, including some fine examples by English, Ger-

man, and French craftsmen. The decorative glassware of the fifteenth to twentieth centuries contains some outstanding specimens of Venetian, Spanish, and German glass.

Mention should also be made of the twelfth-to-seventeeth-century Spanish-Moorish ceramics, especially the exceptionally well-preserved Fortuny Vase, a perfect example of the large decorative vases made in the fourteenth century for the Alhambra. It is named after the Spanish painter Mariano Fortuny, who discovered it near Granada in 1871.

A separaté hall is devoted to some five hundred pieces from the collection of fifteenth-to-eighteenth-

century Italian majolica, enabling us to follow the development of this unique type of ceramics. Particularly rare examples include a dish showing a king seated on his throne, with the signature of the artist, Niccolò Pellipario of Castel Durante (the present Urbania) in Italy, and the date, 1521. The sixteenth-century wedding cups, especially the one depicting Camilla Bella (1537), are also treasures of their kind. In addition, there is a good collection of French Renaissance ceramics and seventeenth- and eighteenth-century French and Dutch (Delft) faïence, including both painted dishes and exquisite figurines.

There is not space enough to mention all the many

celains from 1710, when its production began, to well into the nineteenth century. The display features early reddish-brown pieces, tea and coffee sets painted in silver or with landscapes, objects in the Chinese style, and a multitude of delicate figurines of the middle and late eighteenth century, some reproducing paintings or drawings popular at the time. Especially interesting are the bust of a child made in "red paste," one of the earliest Meissen works (1710–15), and a large ninety-seven-centimeter-high figure of St. Peter, made in 1732 after a model by Johann Gottlieb Kirchner. The so-called St. Andrew Service was ordered from Meissen in 1760 by Empress Elizabeth; composed of 527

and varied types of Western European applied art at the Hermitage, but I cannot leave out the china and porcelain totaling about fourteen thousand pieces, including fine collections of Italian, Spanish, Austrian, Hungarian, Dutch, Danish, and Swedish porcelain of the eighteenth and nineteenth centuries. There are also palace dinner services, decorative vases, inkstands, and so on, as well as numerous figurines from German, French, and English factories.

The museum's collection of Meissen includes por-

pieces, it is decorated with the symbols of the Order of St. Andrew and the coat of arms of Russia.

Sèvres ware is represented by the Green Service (1756), and by the Dessert Service that, ordered by Catherine the Great in 1778–79, is decorated with blue and gold and the empress's monogram. Part of this service was destroyed in the Winter Palace fire of 1837. The collection of Sèvres figurines includes a great number of both colored and white (biscuit) pieces.

Auguste Rodin.
Cupid and Psyche, 1905.
Marble. Height 26 cm, length 67 cm.
From the Sergei Yeliseev collection; in the Hermitage since 1923.

175

1

est tapestries date from the first quarter of the sixteenth century and were woven either in France or at
Brussels.

The most interesting include three series:
Story of the Sablon Madonna, based on cartoons by Ber-
naert van Orley and probably made in a French monastery workshop, *Story of the Knight of the Swan,* and the
Roman de la Rose. The seventeenth-century series *Story
of Constantine* was made from cartoons by Rubens.
Also on display are numerous examples of eighteenth-
century French tapestries and Gobelins, including the
New Testament series (1712–17), presented by Louis
XV to Peter the Great during one of Peter's European
tours. Among the small number of nineteenth-

APPLIED ART

1, 2. Casket depicting
the Adoration of the Magi.
Champlevé enamel. Height 28 cm,
length 29 cm, width 10 cm.
Limoges, second half of thirteenth
century.
Acquired from the Bazilevsky
collection, 1884.

3. St. Stephen as a deacon.
Reliquary. Silver on wood base,
colored stones, filigree.
Height 42 cm.
France, twelfth century.
Acquired from the Bazilevsky
collection, 1884.

4, 5. Diptych showing the Passion.
Carved ivory. Height 32.5 cm,
width 25 cm. C. 1300.
Acquired from the Bazilevsky
collection, 1884.

6. Lid of a mirror case showing
a game of chess.
Carved ivory. Diam. 8.5 cm.
France, first half of fourteenth
century.
Acquired from the Bazilevsky
collection, 1884.

7. Jean Limosin.
Dish depicting a bear hunt.
Enamel. Length 50 cm,
width 38.6 cm. Limoges, late
sixteenth to early seventeenth
centuries.
Acquired from the Bazilevsky
collection, 1884.

8. Wedding cup showing a young
woman.
The banderole bears the inscription,
"Camilla Bella."
Majolica, polychrome painting,
reddish brown luster. Diam. 24 cm.
Castel Durante (modern Urbania),
Italy, 1537. Lustered in Gubbio,
Italy, by Giorgio Andreoli or the
master "N."
Acquired from the M. P. Botkin
collection, 1920.

2

3

A particularly splendid service that once belonged
to Eugène de Beauharnais dates from the early nineteenth century. Napoleon had the Egyptian Service
made for the Tuileries in 1807, but later presented it
to Alexander I. Another rare piece is the porcelain
showing Catherine the Great surrounded by twenty-
three figures representing the peoples of Russia,
which was made at the Berlin Porcelain Factory in
1772. The prime example of English porcelain is the
Green Frog Service, made for the Chesmen Palace in
Petersburg in 1773–74 and kept at Peterhof; its 952
pieces are decorated with English country scenes and
bear the trademark of a frog on a shield.

The Hermitage collection of Western European
tapestries and fabrics is one of the largest in the world.
The bulk of it is made up of gifts to various czars, acquisitions made during the eighteenth and nineteenth
centuries, and items from the collections of Stieglitz,
Yusupov, Shuvalov, Paskevich, and others. The earli-

century items are a carpet woven in the workshop of
William Morris after a cartoon by Sir Edward Burne-
Jones, and *The Fairy Stair* after cartoons by the Belgian
artist Frans Masereel.

The exhibition halls and the storerooms of the
Hermitage contain much fine furniture, both sets and
single pieces. The number of pieces on display is rather small, however; the greater part of the collection is
kept in storage and so is rarely accessible to visitors.
The same is true of the eighteenth- and nineteenth-
century carriages, including one bought by Catherine
the Great in Paris in 1762, and one painted by the
French artist Gravelot and presented to the empress in
1765 by Count Orlov.

Of special value is the medieval and Renaissance
furniture, including French pieces of the seventeenth

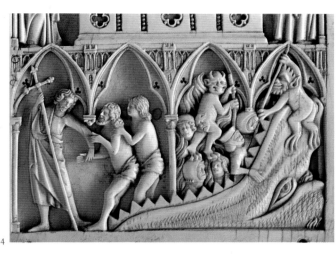

4

5

7

6

8

177

1

and eighteenth centuries. There are rare examples of work by André Charles Boulle and other well-known French cabinetmakers such as Charles Cressant, Jacques Dubois, Bernard Van Riesenburg, and Jean-Henri Riesener. Also of interest is the collection of Roentgen furniture, largely made on order for Catherine the Great.

Along with the furniture, splendid mosaic tabletops made in the baroque style by unknown seventeenth-century craftsmen embellish the Hermitage's halls. One exceptional example, the mosaic *The Sea Bottom,* dates from 1760. Worth special mention is a set of mosaics, particularly the *Views of Rome at Differ-*

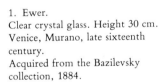

1. Ewer.
Clear crystal glass. Height 30 cm.
Venice, Murano, late sixteenth century.
Acquired from the Bazilevsky collection, 1884.

2. Vase with eight handles.
Clear green glass. Height 17 cm.
Spain, sixteenth century.
Transferred from the Stieglitz Museum, 1923.

3. Duplessis flower vase.
Porcelain. Height 25 cm.
Vincennes, c. 1750.
Acquired from the A.S. Dolgorukov collection, 1918.

4. Serving bowl from the Green Frog Service.
Height 34.5 cm. Wedgwood, 1773–74.
Commissioned by Catherine the Great for the Chesmen Palace in Petersburg.

5. Incense burner.
Silver. Height 40.9 cm.
Maker's mark "J. B."
England, seventeenth century.
Purchased in 1937.

ent Times of Day, by Barberi, a well-known Italian specialist of the early nineteenth century. The Hermitage mosaics also include earlier examples from the thirteenth century on.

Finally, to end this brief survey of Western European works in the Hermitage, I should mention the glyptics, jewelry, and objets d'art. The collection of carved stones (intaglios and cameos), now amounting to over 10,500 items, was begun in the second half of the eighteenth century with the purchase of the famous collections of the Duke of Orleans, the French diplomat Breteuil, Casanova, and others. In this way the museum acquired the cameos that once belonged to the great Rubens.

Older traditions are represented by a small group of thirteenth- and fourteenth-century stones cut by French and Italian craftsmen. There are some priceless fifteenth- and sixteenth-century intaglio portraits, especially those of Francesco Sforza, "Laura la Bella," and Henry II of France. The collection includes numerous works by the English artists Charles and William Brown, who worked on commission for the imperial court. The eighteenth- and nineteenth-century portrait miniatures, executed in various techniques, belonged to the royal collection and had been either commissioned or received as gifts.

The Special Storeroom contains an impressive collection of jewelry with miniatures in enamel. One of the halls of this storeroom, very popular with visitors, displays works by jewelers and goldsmiths from the sixteenth to early nineteenth centuries. Among the sixteenth-century pendants are two pieces fashioned as caravels to commemorate the epic sea voyages of the Spanish navigators of the time. The hull of the first is made out of a single crescent-shaped baroque pearl; set in gold, it has brightly colored enamel ornamentation. The second pendant, somewhat simpler in design, has a hull made of a particularly beautiful Columbian emerald.

One pendant of red spinel (a kind of ruby) takes us back to fabled El Dorado and the discovery in America of new territories abounding in gold and precious stones. Engraved on its gold mount is a caravel bearing the name of Sir Francis Drake, who helped destroy the Spanish Armada in 1588. Works of the sixteenth and seventeenth centuries are represented by precious bowls and goblets made of rock crystal or colored glass, frequently set in gold. Two particularly interesting pieces are a stone pitcher and a washbasin of mid-seventeenth-century Italian manufacture, used by Czar Alexei Mikhailovich.

Watches hung on a chain from the belt became fashionable in the sixteenth century, while seventeenth-century watch cases were richly decorated with gold and jewels; later, watch cases were enameled, sometimes with miniature genre paintings. The eighteenth century is well represented by snuffboxes, then much in vogue as gifts: they come from all over and exhibit every shape and form. Some are carved from a single stone, while others are solid gold studded with precious stones. Several of the splendid snuffboxes on display were produced in Petersburg itself by the jewelers Scharf and Ador.

Many jewelers from other countries worked in Russia, among whom Empress Elizabeth's own jeweler, Jeremiah Posier, was outstanding. In the 1750s there was a rage for small bouquets of flowers made of precious stones and set in vases of rock crystal to create the impression of real water.

Also of interest in the Special Storeroom display are the horses' trappings that the Turkish sultan presented to Nicholas I; the saddlecloths are decorated with gold and countless tiny diamonds. Another noteworthy item is the miniature version of the imperial regalia with crown, orb, and scepter, fashioned by Fabergé for the 1900 World's Fair in Paris.

Hostess.
Porcelain. Model by
Johann Joachim Kaendler.
Height 16 cm. Meissen, c. 1755.
Purchased from Yu. A. Bekman in 1918;
formerly in the F. I. Paskevich
collection.

David Garrick (?) as Richard III.
Porcelain. Height 29.1 cm.
England, Chelsea-Derby factory,
c. 1775.
Acquired in 1921.

Western European porcelain
display in the Great Chapel
of the Winter Palace.
On the right is a statue of
St. Peter.
Porcelain. Height 97 cm. Model by
Johann Gottlieb Kirchner. Meissen,
1732. Transferred from the Museum
of the Society for Encouraging the Arts,
1919.

Exhibition of tapestries in the Ministerial Passage.

Cameo: Joseph and His Brothers.
Sardonyx. 5 × 6.5 cm (minus frame).
Italy, thirteenth century (?).
Acquired from the William Hamilton collection; in the
Rubens collection in the seventeenth century.

Cabinet inlaid with tortoise shell, brass, and
stained horn, with gilded bronze mounts.
André Charles Boulle workshop, c. 1700.
Height 175 cm, length 142 cm, width 54 cm.
Acquired in 1931; formerly in the Sheremetev collection.

Pendant in the form of a caravel.
Emerald in gold setting with enamel decoration and
a cross of five emeralds. Length 10 cm.
Spain, first half of sixteenth century.
In the Winter Palace collection since the eighteenth
century.

181

2

3

4

5

6

7

1. Plate with the painting *Breakfast* after Gabriel Metsu, from the Eugène de Beauharnais Service.
Porcelain. Paris, Dihl et Guérard factory, 1810–14.

2. Pendant in the form of a caravel. Made of an irregularly shaped pearl set in gold filigree studded with rubies and emeralds.
Length 4.5 cm.
Italy, sixteenth century.

3. Pendant made of spinel bearing the inscription: "Fran Drackh. A/1590."
4 × 2.8 cm.
England, late sixteenth century.

4. Bouquet of chrysolites.
Height 24.3 cm.
Petersburg, c. 1740.
In the Winter Palace collection since the eighteenth century.

5. Washbasin made of amethyst.
31.2 × 28.2 cm.
Italy, mid-seventeenth century.
Acquired from the Dmitri Tatishchev collection, 1845.

6. Snuffbox by Jean-Pierre Ador with an allegory on the capture of Bendery (Moldavia) on September 16, 1770.
Height 3.6 cm, diam. 7.3 cm.
Petersburg, early 1770s.
In the Winter Palace collection since the eighteenth century.

7. Snuffbox by Johann Gottlieb Scharf adorned with a bouquet of turquoise and diamonds.
Height 1.5 cm, diam. 6.1 cm.
Petersburg, 1781.
In the Winter Palace collection since the eighteenth century.